Basic DCC Wiring
for Your Model Railroad

Mike Polsgrove

KALMBACH BOOKS

About the author

Mike Polsgrove has been writing *Model Railroader* magazine's "DCC Corner" column since 2003. He has a Bachelor of Science degree in electrical engineering from the Milwaukee School of Engineering and has worked as the motive power electrical engineer for two railroads. Since 1989 he has been designing digital electronic circuits for Eagle Test Systems.

Mike has been a model railroader since the 1960s, and he is currently building an HO layout based on the early 1960s Soo Line. *Basic DCC Wiring for Your Model Railroad* is his third book.

Kalmbach Books
21027 Crossroads Circle
Waukesha, Wisconsin 53186
www.Kalmbach.com/Books

Published in 2011
22 21 20 19 18   7 8 9 10 11

Manufactured in the United States of America

ISBN: 978-0-89024-793-8

Publisher's Cataloging-In-Publication Data

Polsgrove, Mike.

Basic DCC wiring for your model railroad / Mike Polsgrove.

p. ill. (chiefly col.) ; cm. -- (Model railroader books)

"A beginner's guide to decoders, DCC systems, and layout wiring"--Cover.

ISBN: 978-0-89024-793-8

1. Railroads--Models. 2. Railroads--Models--Design and construction. 3. Digital control systems. I. Title. II. Series: Model railroader books.

TF197 .P67 2011

625.1/9

Getting started with DCC

Digital Command Control allows multiple operators to run their trains independently without worrying about electrical blocks or power assignments. This scene is on David Popp's N scale Naugatuck Valley layout.

Digital Command Control (DCC) offers many advantages in operating large and small model railroads alike, namely that you and other modelers are free to run trains independently, without worrying about electrical blocks. DCC also opens up a world of other options, including locomotive sound effects as well as lighting effects on locomotives, passenger cars, and cabooses.

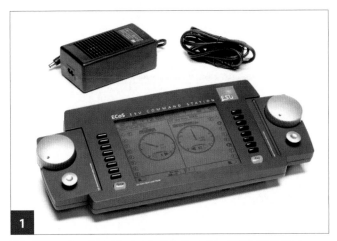

1

This DCC system from Electronic Solutions Ulm (ESU) features a command station with two built-in throttles and an LCD display.

2

Staging Ya...
breaker b...

Label all wires, terminal strips, and connections. You can make notes directly on the benchwork.

Layout wiring is also simplified compared to standard DC cab control, without the need for centralized control panels and dozens of toggle or rotary switches to route power from multiple power packs.

Wiring your model railroad for DCC isn't difficult, but it's something that has to be done correctly to ensure operational reliability, achieve the full benefit of DCC, and most importantly, function safely.

Decoder installation has become much easier in recent years, with plug-in and circuit-board (drop-in-replacement) decoders available for most model locomotives. A number of models are also available with decoders (and even sound decoders) factory installed.

In the following chapters, you'll learn what a DCC system is and how to wire your track, throttles, and turnouts. If you're new to DCC, you'll want to start with Chapter 1 to get a feel for what DCC does. If you're already familiar with the basics of DCC, you can skip ahead to Chapter 2.

Here are a few tips to consider whether you are wiring a DCC or standard DC layout.

Color-code it!

This applies to whatever type of wiring you install. Determine a wiring color code and stick with it. For instance, for my track power I use red for the north rail and black for the south rail. This applies to the entire railroad so the two wires will never get mixed up. It's better to wait until you can get the proper wire and wire it correctly than to wire

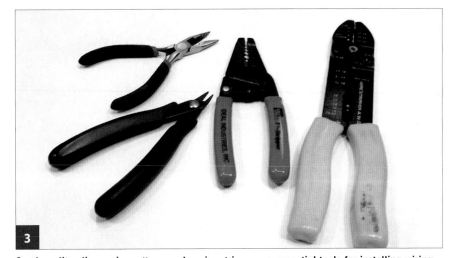

3

Good-quality pliers, wire cutters, and a wire stripper are essential tools for installing wiring.

something in a hurry and make a mistake that you'll be living with for years.

Document it!

Color coding goes a long way toward helping you understand the wiring you did five years ago, but even with that I have found myself staring at an area of my wiring to figure out what I had done years earlier. I've been a member of clubs that had three-ring binders of schematics of every circuit on the layout. In a club environment, that's a must.

For my home layout, I have a combination of formal documentation and notes written under the benchwork. It's easy to take a marker and note what specific wires or terminal strips do rather than trying to guess later.

Get high-quality tools!

You'll need a soldering iron, digital mul-

timeter, wire strippers and needle-nose pliers (more on these in Chapter 1). There's a saying that quality is remembered long after the price is forgotten. This is certainly true with tools. Spend an extra dollar or two for good tools, because you'll regret a low-quality tool every time you use it.

Keep wiring neat!

Neat wiring pays off in several ways. The first is that it makes it easier to install: There is no confusion as to which wire goes where. Secondly, using wire ties to bundle wires helps strain-relieve the whole group. The force of a tug on one wire is distributed to the whole group, lessening the tug on any one wire making it less likely to be damaged. Lastly, it is much easier to trace wiring when troubleshooting a problem.

Let's move on and take a look at the various components of a DCC system.

CHAPTER ONE

What is DCC?

Cody Grivno and David Popp run their trains on Kalmbach Publishing Co.'s Milwaukee, Racine & Troy club layout. DCC allows them to each operate a train independently on the same stretch of track.

Digital Command Control (DCC) is a system for controlling two or more trains on the same track without the multiple electrically isolated sections (blocks) normally needed for conventional DC cab control.

DCC waveform

In the USA, 60-Hertz, 120-volt household current looks like this:

60 Hz AC household current

DCC pulse-width-modulated square wave

"1" bit   "0" bit   Waves not drawn to scale

DCC system overview

Throttle

Sends inputs

Command station

Digital signal

Booster

Digital signal and power to run train

Decoder-equipped loco responds

DCC

DCC signals are much faster (higher frequency) but at a much lower voltage than household AC. DCC sends a series of "ones" and "zeros," the language of computers, by varying the frequency of the waveform. A "one" completes a cycle in 116 microseconds; the "zero" completes its cycle between 190 and 19800 microseconds.

The drawing above shows the basic setup of a DCC system. Small circuit boards (decoders) in each locomotive interpret signals sent through the rails by a command station. Throttles (cabs) send instructions to the command station, with multiple throttles allowing several trains and locomotives to operate at the same time.

Command control is not new. From the 1960s through the 1990s, several analog command control systems were produced, but none ever achieved widespread acceptance because each was proprietary—once a system was purchased, the modeler was limited to products produced by that manufacturer.

That's what makes DCC different. The communication method between the DCC system and the decoders onboard the locomotives is a National Model Railroad Association (NMRA) standard, ensuring compatibility between components of different DCC manufacturers and encouraging competition, which reduces cost.

Further, since DCC uses digital communication, it is extremely flexible

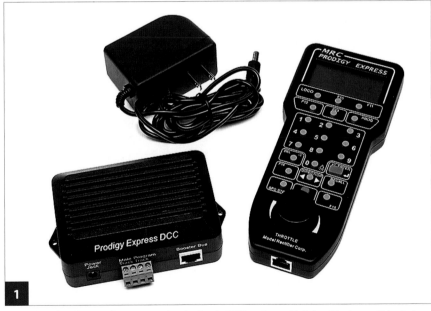

1

MRC's Prodigy Express is an example of a basic DCC system with lots of features. It includes a throttle (right), command station/booster (left), and power supply (top).

and its features can grow as technology advances. Things that haven't even been thought of today can be reality tomorrow.

Model railroad clubs also benefit. A club can choose any brand of DCC system for its layout without forcing

individual club members to choose a specific brand of locomotive decoders. Club members' locomotives will run equally as well on their home DCC systems, even if they are from different manufacturers.

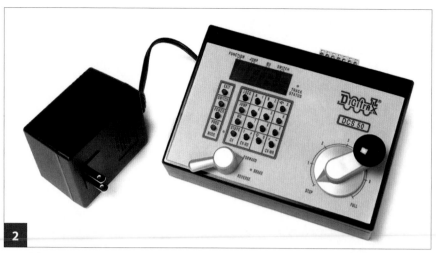

2

The Digitrax Zephyr is an example of a complete DCC system (throttle, command station, and booster) in a single box. The power supply (left) plugs directly into a wall outlet. You can also add other throttles besides the one built into the box.

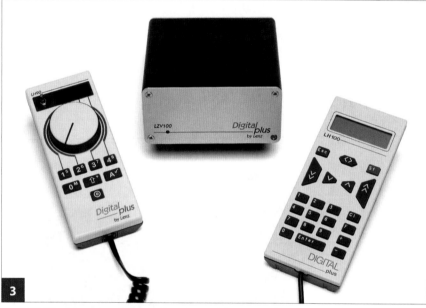

3

The LZV100 command station from Lenz (center) is shown with the LH90 dial-control cab (left) and LH100 push-button master cab (right).

It's not hard to get started in DCC. All that's needed is a DCC system and at least one decoder-equipped locomotive. Many manufacturers offer DCC systems, including Bachmann, CVP Products, Digitrax, Lenz, Model Rectifier Corp. (MRC), North Coast Engineering (NCE), Power Systems Inc. (PSI), and others. All of them are good; you just need to find the right system for your layout. Depending on your budget, layout size, type of operation, and technical expertise, there is a DCC system that will fit your needs (**1, 2, 3, 4**).

A DCC system can be considered an investment. Should you decide to build

another layout or change scales, the DCC system can be reused. If the system allows it, the addition of a few components will allow you to use the same DCC system originally purchased for an N scale layout on an O scale layout.

The cost varies widely with the capability of the system. Smaller systems can usually only run a few trains and start for under $200. Larger systems are expandable, and by adding more throttles and boosters can grow to meet the needs of the largest layouts.

DCC systems consist of several components. They can be in separate boxes or all in one unit. Most makers offer

starter systems that include everything you need to get up and running. Individual components of the DCC system are generally not interchangeable between manufacturers. However, a DCC system can control locomotives with decoders from other manufacturers.

Throttles or cabs

The throttle is the part of a DCC system you'll use the most. Some people prefer the term throttle and some prefer cab; either way, this is the device with which operators actually control the trains. At the minimum, it contains some sort of speed and direction controls (just like a DC power pack), but with DCC additional controls are usually present. The most common of these is function control, usually in the form of push buttons that control headlights and ditch lights. If your locomotive is sound equipped, functions also control the bell, whistle, and other effects.

Every DCC manufacturer makes at least one throttle to work with its DCC system—some are simple and some are more complex, **5**. Some have throttles built into the command station. Other throttles are handheld and either tethered to the layout or wireless.

Most DCC manufacturers have more than one style of throttle, but with few exceptions, throttles will work only on each manufacturer's systems only. CVP, the maker of EasyDCC, makes throttles that are compatible through an adapter with Lenz DCC systems. Atlas throttles are also compatible with Lenz systems. For their wireless throttles, Lenz uses ordinary cordless phones.

The Digitrax Zephyr system has a unique capability called "jump" ports that allow you to reuse your DC power packs as DCC throttles by connecting them to the DCC system.

Finding a throttle you are comfortable with is one of the major factors in choosing a DCC system. After all, this is the part of your system you'll be using the most. Knobs, thumbwheels, and push buttons are the most common methods for controlling locomotive speed. Some throttles have directional toggle switches, some have buttons, and some use the same knob that controls the speed to control the direction. On those

This is the Bachmann E-Z Command Dynamis system. The handheld controller (left) is wireless, and it communicates with the base station via infrared signals. The controller has a joystick for control and an LCD display screen.

There are many styles of DCC throttles. Make sure the system you purchase has a style of throttle with which you are comfortable. From left to right are an NCE Procab, Cab 04PR wireless for NCE's Powerhouse Pro, a Digitrax wireless, and an Easy DCC (CVP) tethered cab.

throttles, turning the knob to the right of center makes the locomotive move forward; turning it to the left causes the locomotive to move in reverse.

Command station

The command station is the "brains" of a DCC system. It can be a stand-alone box or it can be combined into one unit with other components such as a booster and throttle. Some systems have the command station built into a tethered throttle.

The command station receives instructions from the throttle over the cab bus (more about the cab bus in cab bus section), or in the case of built-in throttles, directly from the throttle on the command station. These instructions are converted to DCC signals that are sent to the booster. The capabilities of the system are determined by the command station. These include the maximum number of throttles allowed, how many trains can be run at the same time, and a

host of other things. If your DCC system is so equipped, it also contains terminals to connect a programming track.

Booster

The booster increases the power of the DCC signal so that it can supply the digital signal to the rails with enough power to run multiple locomotives. Boosters are often packaged together with the command station but are also available separately. Multiple boosters

Glossary of DCC terms

Accessory decoder. Decoder that provides power and operational control of one or more layout accessory devices. Do not install an accessory decoder in a locomotive. Accessory decoders are intended for operating layout accessories such as turnouts, signals, animation devices, lighting, etc. Also known as a stationary decoder.

Address. The address is used by the command station to communicate with a specific decoder. It can be either two- or four-digit, depending on the system, and is typically part of the locomotive's road number. Addresses are unique to each decoder.

Alternating current (AC). An electric current that reverses its direction of flow at regular intervals. Each move from zero to maximum strength and back to zero is half a cycle. A full cycle includes excursions in both the positive and negative direction.

Ammeter. Meter used to measure current strength—for example, how many amps a locomotive draws when it stalls.

Ampere or amp. Unit used to determine the amount of an electrical current.

Automatic reversing. A circuit that senses short circuits and reverses the polarity. Used commonly with reversing loops, wyes, and turntables.

Block. Section of track that is electrically isolated from the rest of the layout.

Booster. Takes the low-power signal from the command station and "boosts" it to the high-power signal needed by locomotives to operate DC motors, etc., in conformance with NMRA Standard S-9.1. Also referred to as power stations or power boosters.

Cab. Usually a handheld piece of equipment with necessary controls to send speed, direction, and other information to the locomotive. Frequently referred to as "throttle."

Cab bus. Used to connect handheld and stationary cabs to a command station. Wireless cabs are indirectly connected to a cab bus via their companion wireless base.

Circuit. The path of an electrical current.

Circuit breaker. A switch that automatically protects the Digital Command Control system and all the decoders on the layout in the event of a current overload.

Command control. Controlling trains independently of each other. Each locomotive has a decoder or receiver that responds only to its own discrete address.

Command station. The "brains" of the DCC system. It receives information from the cab, forms the appropriate DCC "packet," and transmits this information in an NMRA DCC-compliant signal to the track via the booster.

Configuration variable (CV). A number programmed into a decoder that controls its behavior. These numbers remain stored until they are reprogrammed. An address is an example of a configuration variable.

Consist. A grouping of locomotives controlled as if they were one. Consisting allows several locos to be connected together to pull a long train up a steep grade. Also known as "MU-ing" (from multiple units). With basic consisting, the command station sends the same commands to each loco in the consist. With advanced consisting, each decoder-equipped locomotive responds to the address of the consist, enabling the command station to control the consist with a single command.

Consist address. The address to which all digital decoders in a consist respond.

Control bus. A cable connecting the command station to its boosters.

Decoder. A small circuit board that receives digital packets of information addressed to it by the command station in accordance with the NMRA standards. Mobile decoders are mounted inside locomotives and control the motor, lights, and sounds. Accessory decoders are used to control non-locomotive items such as turnout motors and signals.

Digital Command Control (DCC). Method of controlling multiple trains and accessories using digital communications packets to send commands.

Direct current (DC). Electrical current that flows in only one direction. Used for control of most model railroads before command control.

DPDT. Double-pole, double-throw. Switch used on model railroads to allow you to change the polarity of the current for reverse loops or for complex block control. Some DPDT switches have a "center-off" feature.

Fixed cab. A cab or throttle permanently mounted to one location.

Function buttons. Buttons on a throttle that control locomotive accessories such as lighting and sound.

Function mapping. Changing a decoder's CVs to determine which function button controls which function output.

Function outputs. Wires on a decoder that power locomotive accessories such as lighting. Function outputs are most commonly used to control sound effects and the front and rear headlights of a locomotive.

Instruction packets. The regular packet format used for most commands.

Operations mode programming. Also known as "programming on the main." Changing the CVs of an individual locomotive on a track other than the programming track. Not all decoders or DCC systems support this.

Packet. The sequence of bits used to encode the instructions upon which a decoder operates.

Power district. An area of the layout connected directly to its own booster, electrically isolated from any other boosters or power districts.

Power supply. Converts household AC into low-voltage DC to power a DCC system.

Programming track. A short piece of track electrically separated from the main trackage. It is used to program any CV, including the decoder's address. CVs may also be read back to the cab from a decoder on the programming track.

Pulse-width modulation (PWM). Used to control the speed of a DC motor by applying pulses of a constant voltage of varying width. The wider the pulses, the faster the motor turns. This is the method of motor control used by DCC decoders.

Rectifier. A device inside a decoder for converting electrical AC current into DC current.

Resistor. Restricts the flow of electrical current to lower its voltage or limit its current.

SPDT. Single-pole, double-throw. A type of electrical switch used in model railroading.

Speed table. A table of parameters specifying the motor voltage in response to a speed and direction command. Individual speed tables can be programmed for each locomotive, allowing locomotives from different manufacturers to work together in a consist.

Track bus. Heavy-gauge copper wire used to distribute the electrical power from the booster around the layout. Each booster has its own set of track bus wires. Accessory decoders may be connected to a track bus. The wire gauge of a track bus must be appropriate to the rating of the associated power station and load.

Track feeders. Used to attach the track bus wires to the track. Track feeders are usually smaller in diameter, such as 22 gauge.

Transformer. Changes high-voltage 110-volt AC house current into low-voltage AC current to power your DCC system.

Volt. A unit of electrical potential. Commonly, 0 to 9 volts of DC are used for Z scale, 0 to 14 volts DC for N and HO scale, and 0 to 20 volts DC for large-scale model railroading.

Walkaround cab. A cab or throttle that is handheld and connected by a cable to a plug connected to the cab bus at multiple points around the layout. Memory-equipped walkaround cabs allow a train to maintain speed and direction while the cab is unplugged from the cab bus.

Wireless cab. A handheld cab that has no cable connection to the layout. Wireless cabs use infrared or radio waves as a method of transmitting information.

Wireless cab base. A base station for one or more wireless cabs. Connected to the command station via a cab bus.

6

Several types of decoders are available, including (clockwise from top), a Digitrax plug-style next to an HO scale Kato SD40, an Atlas dual-mode circuit-board decoder next to an Atlas GP40-2, and an NCE circuit-board decoder designed as a drop-in for a Proto 2000 GP7.

are often needed for large layouts that require more power (more about that in Chapter 3). Sometimes boosters from different manufacturers can be mixed on the same layout.

Transformers/power supplies

Boosters (and often command stations) require an external transformer or power supply. Transformers take household AC power and step it down to lower voltage. Power supplies not only step the voltage down, but rectify it to DC.

Each DCC manufacturer has its own requirements for a transformer/power supply to power their equipment. These requirements must be strictly adhered to or damage may occur. Virtually all DCC components use DC as their final source of power before converting it to a DCC signal, but many have built-in rectifiers so they can use either AC or DC for input. In those systems, you might find it

less expensive to use an AC transformer rather than a DC power supply.

The DCC system or booster will generally rate its input in terms of a voltage range and a minimum current. The voltage of the transformer/power supply must be within the limits, but the current rating is the minimum. It is OK to have a transformer/power supply with a current rating above what is required, but not below.

Most DCC manufacturers offer power supplies or transformers that are compatible with their equipment.

Decoders

Decoders are the last items needed to run a DCC layout. Unlike other system components, almost any DCC decoder can be controlled by any DCC system.

Decoders vary widely in complexity, capacity, and physical size, **6**. The simplest decoders are the ones that come factory

installed. Many newer locomotives are available with OEM (original equipment manufacturer) decoders, **7**. These often come with sound and are ready to go after programming them to a unique decoder address. (See more about programming decoders in Chapter 6.)

Some locomotives are advertised as "DCC ready." This ambiguous phrase can mean a couple of things. For many current locomotives, it means that the model comes equipped with a socket, allowing any number of decoders to simply be plugged into place. Read the specifications carefully, as sometimes "DCC Ready" just means that the basic DCC preparation is done (the motor is isolated from the frame), but some soldering or hand wiring will be required to add a decoder.

The NMRA specifies a number of standard connectors with which DCC manufacturers equip their decoders.

Along with plug-equipped decoders, some manufactures offer specialized "drop-in" decoders that are designed to replace the circuit board in specific locomotives. Some models—especially N scale locomotives and switchers in larger scales—have so little spare room under the shell that a drop-in decoder is often the best choice if one is available.

Some decoders must be directly wired to the locomotive. These have standard color-coded wires that are soldered to the motor, the track pick-ups, and lights, **8**. These require a little more skill to install than drop-in or plug decoders, but are sometimes the only choice if no drop-in is available. This is often the case when adding decoders to older locomotives. Also, you may desire some of the motor control properties, specific sounds, or lighting effects offered by a certain decoder.

There's quite a variety of sound decoders available as well. Many models now come with factory-installed sound, and separate sound decoders are available in plug-in, drop-in, and wired versions as well. There are also sound decoders that don't include motor controls. These allow you to use your favorite motor controller or add one to a locomotive already equipped with a motor decoder. Some sound decoders have generic steam or diesel sounds, others are programmed with a specific locomotive's sound, and some can be modified by downloading various sound files. Just about all sound decoders allow you to modify the horn and whistle sounds.

Some companies offer sound decoders that can have the sounds modified by downloading. These require a computer and specialized hardware. These manufacturers usually have a number of pre-made sound projects on their websites, or sometimes you can make your own.

DCC system features

Optional features of DCC systems include long or short addressing, fine-speed motor control, and sound.

Long addressing (sometimes called four-digit) is a feature that must be found on the DCC command station and the decoder used as well. This is the ability to go past 127 locomotive addresses. On some DCC systems anything above

Many locomotive models are available with DCC decoders already installed. This **HO scale Proto 2000 GP9** has a factory-installed QSI sound system with speaker.

Along with motor control, decoders have extra outputs called functions. These are being used to control headlights, ditchlights, and a rooftop beacon on this **HO scale SD40**.

address 99 is considered a long address, hence the separation between two-digit and four-digit addressing. To match your locomotives' DCC addresses with their road numbers, consider long addressing. On most, if not all, DCC systems that support long addresses, you can combine decoders using short addresses and those using long addresses on the same layout.

Fine-speed motor control is a feature offered on many decoders to help with

low-speed operation. Some decoders have a variable-pulse method of controlling the locomotive's motor similar to DC pulse-power packs, and others employ a method called back-electro-motive force (BEMF). This uses the characteristic of DC motors of generating a voltage while rotating. The decoder measures this voltage and determines the locomotive's speed, fine tuning its output to keep the locomotive at a constant speed.

CHAPTER TWO

Track wiring

Keeping below-table wires neat is a key to reliable track-bus wiring. Label wires and use wire ties or holes in the benchwork to route the wires.

In theory, since isolated electrical blocks are not required to run multiple trains with DCC, all that would be needed to supply the needed power your layout would be a single pair of track feeder wires. In practice, however, it's not quite that simple. Although DCC wiring is simpler than multi-cab DC wiring, you'll need more than a pair of track feeders to ensure reliable operation.

Wiring tools include a soldering iron and resin-core solder, pliers, wire cutters, and wire strippers. The brown and red suitcase connectors allow for solderless wire connections. Wire comes in different colors and gauges.

Wire is either stranded (left) or solid. Stranded wire is more flexible than solid.

Wire is available in a wide variety of colors. Color-coding all wire on your layout will make adding future accessories and trouble-shooting any problems much easier tasks.

Once a DCC signal is produced by the command station and amplified by the booster, it needs to get to the rails. Because this output runs multiple trains at the same time, DCC boosters must supply a lot of current, much more than a conventional DC power pack. To get that current to the rails safely, a properly wired track bus with multiple feeder wires is needed.

One reason is electrical resistance. The nickel-silver rail of most model railroad track is actually a pretty poor conductor of electricity—that is, nickel-silver rail has a large resistance to flow of electricity. The larger the resistance, the more voltage drop there is for a given length the rail. The relation is called Ohm's Law.

Ohm's Law states that Voltage = Current x Resistance ($V = IR$, where V = volts, I = current in amps and R = resistance in ohms). Where the current remains the same and there is more resistance, the more voltage is lost.

To test this, I measured a sample of HO scale code 83 nickel-silver rail and found its resistance to be .057 ohms per foot. As an example, the main line of my HO scale Soo Line layout is about 120 feet long. If the layout were fed by a single pair of track feeders at one end and I ran a three-locomotive train drawing an average of 250 milliamps (mA, or .250 amps) per locomotive to the other end of the layout, the voltage would drop about 10 volts! (240 feet of rail—the distance out and back—is 13.68 ohms.) The total current of three locomotives is .75 amps. Given that my DCC system is nominally 14 volts, that would leave only 4 volts to run the decoders and the trains. Not only is that well below the NMRA minimum standard of 7 volts, it's simply not enough to run HO locomotives. Also consider that more than one train would be running at one time, and in reality the voltage drop would even be worse.

Unsoldered rail joiners provide even more resistance than the rails alone. The exact amount depends on how tightly they fit and whether they make good contact with the base of each rail (which is sometimes weathered or painted).

It also simply isn't safe to wire a layout this way. Many DCC boosters are capable of supplying a large amount of current, as much as 10 amps for some systems. Boosters are equipped with circuit breakers that trip in case of a short circuit. However, with a large amount of resistance in the track, a short circuit at the far end might not be detected by the booster. The result is the full current of the booster passing through the short circuit. If the short circuit happens to be in the form of a brass locomotive truck, it could easily be melted or worse, start a fire.

The solution to voltage loss is to add a track bus under the benchwork. This consists of two heavy wires parallel to the track that are connected to the rails by smaller feeder wires. How heavy the wire needs to be depends on the length of the bus and the current load on it.

Wire

Wire comes in different sizes called gauges. In the United States, a number followed by AWG (American Wire Gauge) designates size: the larger the gauge number, the lighter (smaller in diameter) the wire. The heavier the wire, the less resistance it has and the less voltage drop will occur for a given amount of current.

The most common wire sizes for track buses are No. 12 AWG and No. 14 AWG. Number 12 wire has a DC resistance of .00156 ohms per foot and No. 14 has a DC resistance of .0025 ohms per foot. The DCC signal is technically AC, so there is an additional AC resistance (called reactance) due to something called "skin effect," but skin effect is largely negligible for our purposes. The DC resistance of the bus is a close estimation of the overall impedance.

Back to my example of a 120-foot main line: A track bus with No. 14 AWG wire would have a resistance of .66 ohms; with a three-unit train that's a drop of .45 volts. I placed my booster in the middle of the bus, which results in two shorter buses and lowers the drop to .225 volts.

In reality, more than one train is usually running throughout the layout, so the current draw is higher. The exact voltage drop depends on how many locomotives are running and exactly where they are on the layout.

Another way to reduce the voltage drop is to use heavier wire. If I used No.

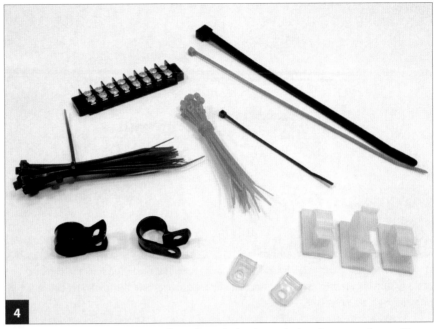

4

Barrier terminal strips (top) and various sizes of wire ties and wire clamps can be used to bundle wire to keep under-layout wiring neat and organized.

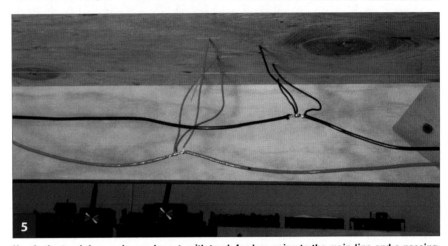

5

Here's the track bus under my layout, with track feeders going to the main line and a passing siding. Note that the bare portions of the bus where the track feeders are soldered are offset from one another to prevent short circuits should the bus be accidentally bumped.

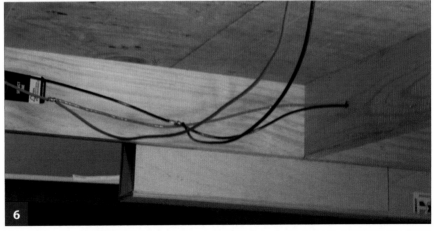

6

This shows a tee in the track bus under a yard. While tees in the bus are permitted, the fewer and shorter they are, the cleaner the DCC signal will be at the tracks.

This shows the track bus wires twisted in the foreground and separated from the cab bus cable toward the rear. To avoid electrical interference, don't route the track and cab bus wires through the same hole.

You may need an extra-long long bit when drilling wire-access holes through roadbed and benchwork. I use ⅛"-diameter bit for No. 22 wire.

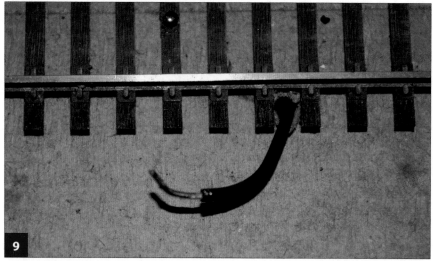

Insert and tin the end of the feeder wire. Putting a slight bend in the wire will allow it to fit snugly against the web of the rail.

12 AWG wire, a split bus would have a resistance of .1872 ohms and the voltage drop of one three-unit train on the farthest point on the layout would be just .140 volts—hardly noticeable.

Another consideration in determining the gauge of your track bus wires is the amount of current the wires can carry without overheating. In most communities in the United States, the electrical code specifies that No. 14 wire can safely be used for loads up to 15 amps and No. 12 wire can safely be used for loads up to 20 amps.

Wire is either solid or stranded. Stranded wire is made of many smaller wires and is far more flexible, whereas solid wire is stiff.

It is essential that you color-code your wiring. I use black wire for the south rail and red wire for the north rail for my track bus, but any colors will do as long as you are consistent.

As previously mentioned, DCC is an AC waveform. Without getting into electrical theory, what this means is that a track bus can act like an antenna, and your DCC system can act like a radio station and interfere with other electronic devices in the area. To reduce interference, some DCC manufacturers recommend twisting bus wires a few times every foot or so. Also, besides the impedance in the length of a wire due to skin effect, a track bus wire also has impedance through its insulation to the other track bus wire. Twisting the wires makes that impedance constant throughout the length of the bus and may help the appearance of the DCC waveform.

Some DCC manufacturers recommend adding an AC filter, snubber, or terminator at the end of the track bus. These consist of resistors and capacitors placed across the bus. These are designed to reduce ringing and overshoot of the DCC waveform, potentially protecting your decoders from damage, but they can also interfere with track occupation detection. Check the manual for your DCC system for details.

If you are running a large number of trains or planning to signal your layout by using track current for train detection, you will need to consider dividing your track bus into several subsections. If more power than a single booster can supply is needed, each booster must have its own power district (more on that in Chapter 3). Also, signal systems incorporating block current detection will require separate blocks.

Track feeders

Once your track bus is in place, it must be connected to the rails. This is done through lighter-gauge wires called track feeders. The size of these feeders depends on the layout scale. For HO, I use No. 22 AWG stranded wire, but even smaller wire will do.

This light-gauge wire is OK for feeders because their short length (6" to 12") doesn't significantly add to the overall voltage drop, and each set of feeders is only carrying a small portion of the overall current carried by the bus. The lighter wire makes feeders easier to solder to track and easier to conceal in ballast.

Color-coding track feeders is also important—use the same colors as the track bus to avoid any confusion.

As discussed earlier, rail joiners alone are extremely poor conductors of electricity. This becomes especially apparent at the higher currents DCC layouts can provide.

Soldering the rail joints is a good way to avoid problems. Clean the rails at the mating joints and solder the joiner in place. However, it's good to leave some joints unsoldered with a slight gap to allow for expansion and contraction of the rail and benchwork components because of changes in heat and humidity.

A better method is to attach a track feeder to each piece of rail. I combine the two methods by adding a track feeder wire to every large section of rail and soldering the rail joiners on very small pieces of rail.

Soldering rail joiners and track feeders requires proper technique. The most important thing is to make sure the mating surfaces are clean. Any dirt, oxidation, or paint (such as weathered rail) will make it virtually impossible to get a neat solder joint. A needle file helps ensure the rail is clean and bare before attempting to solder it. I also use a rosin-based flux to further clean the rail during soldering. Never use acid flux (or acid-

The feeder is placed firmly atop the base of the rail against the web of the rail. Note that the rail in this area has been cleaned with a file to remove paint and weathering.

Apply a dab of solder flux paste to the joint before soldering.

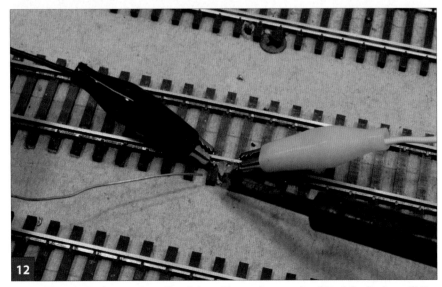

Place the soldering iron on the rail and the solder on the opposite side of the feeder until the solder flows through the joint. The clips keep heat away from the plastic ties.

13

The solder should flow smoothly and the finished joint should have a shiny appearance.

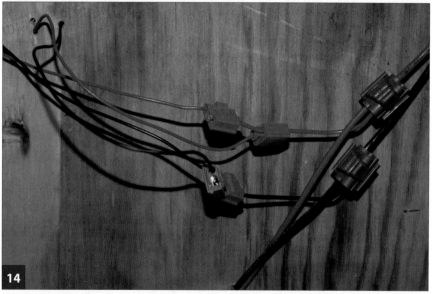

14

On my son Matt's N scale layout I used 3M Scotchlok ("suitcase") connectors to attach the feeders to the track bus. Since there was no one connector that would connect the 22 AWG feeders to the 12 AWG bus, I had to use 18 AWG wires between the two.

core solder) for an electrical joint, as it will eventually corrode.

For smaller rail (code 100 and under), a 40-watt pencil-type soldering iron is perfect. For larger rail (code 125 or above), a larger iron or soldering gun will work. The proper iron allows the joint to be heated quickly enough to allow the solder to flow through the joint but not melt plastic ties.

Another way to prevent melting plastic ties is to use a heat sink on either side of the joint. This prevents the rail on the other side of the heat sink from becoming too hot. I use alligator clips from test clips on my HO layout, but these are too large for rail in smaller scales. Hemostat locking pliers work well for N scale.

Applying a bit of resin flux to the joint before soldering will help the solder flow freely. Heat the joint with the soldering iron and apply solder to the joint—not directly on the soldering iron. The metals being joined must be hot enough to melt the solder so it flows through the joint.

Attaching feeders to the track bus can be done a couple of ways. Soldering this joint requires stripping the insulation

away from the bus and feeder wires and wrapping the track feeder around the bus. A strong mechanical joint is essential before soldering the wire: Don't depend on the solder for holding the wire in place. Stagger the joints so that the feeders for the two different wires don't short to one another should the track bus get bumped. Stripping the bus wires can be done with a knife or—even easier—a jaw-type wire stripper. Many find that using solid wire for the track bus makes stripping the wires easier.

Wrapping soldered joints in electrical tape will minimize the chances of bare wires contacting each other and causing a short circuit.

Soldering under benchwork is not my favorite thing to do, so thankfully there is another method. Insulation deplacement connectors (IDCs, also called suitcase connectors) don't require solder. The insulation does not have to be stripped from either the bus or the track feeder, saving a couple of time-consuming steps.

These connectors have a "run" and a "tap." The run is where the track bus goes through the connector and the tap is where the track feeder terminates in the connector. Several brands are available; I prefer 3M's Scotchlok connectors, as their design offers two places where the metal connector contacts the mating wires.

Place the wires in the IDC, then use pliers to clamp the metal connector in place. Close the plastic flap/cover until it snaps in place, and you're done.

These connectors come in several sizes, with AWG numbers listed for the tap and run. Make sure that you choose the proper connector for the wire sizes you are using. My son's layout uses No. 12 AWG bus wire and No. 22 track feeders. There is no connector of this type that will join these two sizes of wires, so I used an intermediate 18 AWG wire with a large connector to join it to the track bus and a smaller connector to connect it to the track feeders.

To ensure your track is wired safely, place a coin across the rails at various locations on your railroad, including the place farthest from your booster(s). At every location, the circuit breaker must trip. If not, your wiring isn't adequate.

Programming track

As you wire your layout, you should plan a location for a programming track—a section of track dedicated to setting up (programming) your locomotive decoders. The programming track should be a totally isolated section of track on your workbench or a little-used siding on your layout.

Many DCC command stations have a separate output for a programming track. The wires from this output should go directly to the programming track and should never contact the track bus.

If you set up a test track on your workbench as a programming track, you'll still want the track to be connected to your mainline track bus as well. This will allow you to test-run your locomotives as well as program them. The important thing is that the track not be connected to both the main line and the programming terminals of your DCC system at the same time, or the result could be programming every locomotive on your layout at the same time! Worse yet, you may damage your DCC system.

My test track is at my workbench, and I have a rotary switch to select whether my DCC system's mainline or programming terminals power it. A double-pole, double-throw (DPDT) toggle switch will also work.

If you choose to use a spur track on your layout, you should also control the power source with a rotary or toggle switch. When the programming mode is selected, be sure a locomotive or lighted passenger car doesn't bridge the rail gaps between the programming track and the main line.

If you plan to install sound decoders, be aware that many sound decoders draw more current than a typical programming track can supply. Both Soundtraxx and DCC Specialties make programming-track boosters to aid in programming sound decoders. These boosters require an external power supply, but can be permanently wired to your programming track.

There are several brands of sound decoders that allow you to download new sounds into them through the rails. These require a special stand-alone programmer for each brand of decoder. This track needs to be isolated from any other track and your DCC system. I use

Terminal strips and spade connectors help keep wiring neat, as with these circuit breakers and accessory decoders. They also avoid the need to solder under the benchwork.

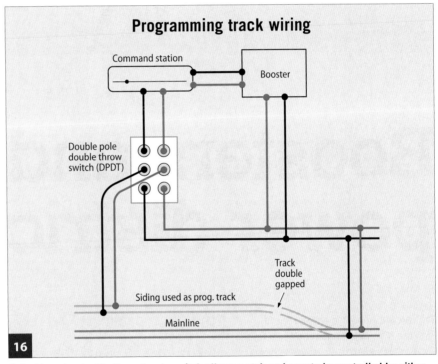

A double-pole, double-throw toggle switch allows a stub-end spur to be controlled by either the programming terminals or the layout's track bus wiring.

the same test track that is on my bench, again using a rotary switch to select which programmer powers my test track.

Lastly, I wired a conventional DC throttle into my rotary switch for testing locomotives prior to installing DCC decoders.

It should be noted that with most DCC systems, decoders can be programmed directly on the main line of your layout. This is called operations-mode programming (or "programming on the main"). This method has distinct advantages over programming on the programming track, especially for programming motor-control CVs. However, except for bi-directional DCC decoders, the values of the CVs currently programmed in the decoder cannot be read back while it is on the main line. We'll cover decoders and decoder programming in Chapter 6.

CHAPTER THREE

Boosters and power districts

You can add more than one booster to increase the available power on your layout. The box on the left is a combined command station and five-amp booster from NCE. The box on the right is a dedicated five-amp booster. A control bus from one to the other sends the DCC commands.

By its very nature, DCC is designed to control more than one train at a time. Thus, the system must supply enough power to run all trains and locomotives in operation. One booster may be enough to power all trains on a small layout, but depending on the scale and number of locomotives you intend to run at once, you may need to add one or more boosters.

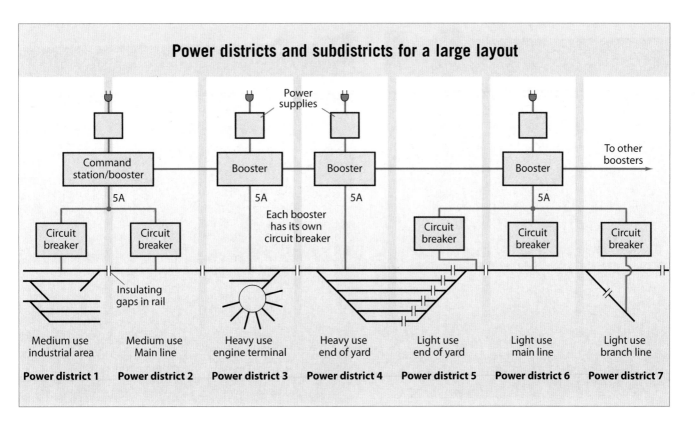

Power districts and subdistricts for a large layout

Power supplies

Command station/booster — Booster — Booster — Booster — To other boosters

5A   5A   5A   5A

Each booster has its own circuit breaker

Circuit breaker (×7)

Insulating gaps in rail

Medium use industrial area	Medium use Main line	Heavy use engine terminal	Heavy use end of yard	Light use end of yard	Light use main line	Light use branch line
Power district 1	**Power district 2**	**Power district 3**	**Power district 4**	**Power district 5**	**Power district 6**	**Power district 7**

Boosters come in several sizes measured or rated by the current (in amperes) they can supply. Booster power ranges from small two- to three-amp versions to large ten-amp models.

It is important to note that if you add a second booster, each booster must provide power to its own section of track, called a power district. The track between power districts must be isolated by a gap in both rails, and the track bus below the benchwork must also be divided.

Determining current draw

To determine if you need to have additional boosters on your layout, add the current draw of everything that is connected to your track bus. This not only includes locomotives but any accessories as well, such as lighting in passenger cars, stationary decoders (more about them later), and signal systems.

Start by adding up locomotive current draw (these are estimates; individual locomotives can draw more or less power). An N scale locomotive typically draws about .25A but can draw .75A under heavy load or if sound equipped, an HO locomotive will draw anywhere from .25A to 1A, and O and large-scale locomotives draw even more. As a general rule, newer locomotives with

can motors draw less current than older locomotives with open-frame motors.

Locomotives draw the most current when they are running and draw very little, even if sound-equipped, while idling. Idle current can be minimized by keeping locomotive lighting off and muting sounds on locomotives not in use.

Passenger car lighting can be another large source of current. A single light bulb can draw 10 to 100 mA.

Stationary decoders (see Chapter 4), signal systems, wayside lighting, or anything else that uses track bus power must be taken into account.

If you add up all the current your DCC system needs to supply and it exceeds the current rating of the booster that came with your DCC system, you'll want to add an additional booster or two.

Be aware that some basic entry-level DCC systems don't have the capability of adding additional boosters. If you think you'll need another booster, carefully check the system specifications (or read the manual online) before purchasing it.

If you discover you need an extra booster or two, you need to determine how to divide your layout into sections—called power districts—to make the most of your boosters and your wiring. The drawing above shows one example of

how a large layout could be divided into power districts with separate boosters and circuit breakers (more on those in a bit).

Splitting the layout into halves or thirds is a logical way to approach the problem, but you might later find you have a particular area that draws a lot of current. For instance, if you have a large intercity passenger depot that hosts multiple trains at once, each of which has several lighted passenger cars, along with platform lighting (connected to the track bus) and stationary decoders, you might choose to dedicate a booster to that area while leaving another single booster to power the rest of the layout. This might balance the power load better.

I've seen multi-level layouts with a different booster for each level and a double-track layout with each track having its own booster. All will work—what is best will depend on what's most efficient for your layout.

My layout is divided into two power districts with two boosters—one powering each district. The boosters are not in the center of the layout, so for a small section of my railroad I have two track buses under the layout.

How boosters are connected to each other and to the command station varies from system to system.

NCE recommends grounding the cases of each booster together. When separate transformers power the boosters, this provides a common voltage reference. Follow the instructions of your system regarding grounding to avoid damaging your equipment or creating a shock hazard.

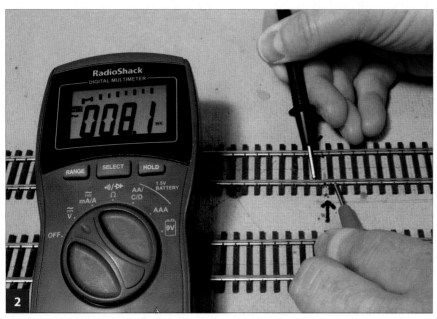

Measure the voltage across the rail gap on the same rail using the AC voltage setting of your digital multimeter. If the boosters are in phase, the voltage will be near zero. This measurement is 8.1 mV (0.0081 volts)—very close to zero.

I recommend that each booster have its own dedicated power supply and that the chassis of the boosters be wired together to provide a common reference point. Always check the manual for your system, and follow the manufacturer's instructions closely.

Booster voltage

When a locomotive passes from one power district to another across the gaps in the rails, it briefly draws power simultaneously from two boosters. Because of this it's best to have the voltage of the track boosters adjusted

as closely as possible to one another. This is not always easy. The DCC signal is a square wave, and although most multimeters do not measure it accurately, using the AC volts setting on your meter will give you a rough idea of the voltage.

The voltage cannot be adjusted on some boosters. For those that do allow it to be adjusted, there is sometimes a test point that allows measuring a DC voltage that represents the DCC signal's AC output. This can easily be measured by a multimeter.

Tony's Train Exchange sells a device called the RRampMeter that is specifically designed to measure DCC voltage, and CVP's manual (available online) shows a circuit consisting of a bridge rectifier, a capacitor, and a resistor that also approximates track voltage.

Boosters that can be adjusted usually have an internal potentiometer (dial). Carefully follow the manufacturer's instructions for this. The process may involve adjusting live circuits with the cover off, so it's best to use non-metallic tools.

Getting boosters in phase

More important than matching the voltage of your boosters is getting them in phase. You must have the same polarity on each rail on either side of the gap separating the two boosters' power districts. This is where color-coding really pays off, as it will reduce wiring errors that lead to boosters being out of phase. To check the phase, put your multimeter on a range adequate to measure 20 volts AC (the exact voltage is not important)

Connect the meter across the gap in the rail that separates power districts. It should measure near zero volts. To double-check, measure across the rails—the meter should read close to your booster voltage. If you get booster voltage across the rail gap, the polarity is reversed on one of the boosters—simply reverse the wiring connections at the booster. If you have more than two boosters, check the phase at every power-district gap.

Some boosters can be set in an auto-reverser mode. These are for wyes and balloon tracks that form reversing

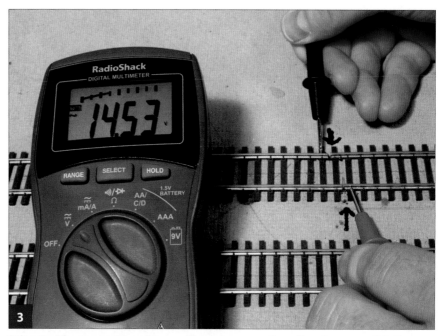

Using the AC voltage setting of your multimeter, measure the voltage from one rail to the other rail on either side of the gaps as indicated by the arrows. The measurement should be close to full track voltage.

Circuit breakers for subdistricts include (clockwise from left) the Digitrax PM42 with four breakers, the NCE EB3 with three breakers, and the Tony's Train Exchange Power Shield with one to four breakers.

sections (more on those in Chapter 4). I recommend turning that feature off unless the booster is actually connected to a reversing section. Otherwise, it can be confusing when trying to get your boosters in phase.

Subdistricts, detection blocks

Once you've determined how many boosters you require, you may want to consider subdividing your track (and track bus) into further subsections.

You may find that a derailment in one location shuts down the section of the layout that is connected to that booster. If you have only one booster, it shuts down the entire layout. The same is true if you run through an open turnout. In fact, if your layout is wired sufficiently, any short circuit will cause the breaker on the booster to trip.

If you have multiple operators, this can become very annoying. Your train may suddenly stop, and it might take

5 This **NCE EB3** circuit breaker is mounted to one of the legs of my layout benchwork. The track bus from the booster comes in from the bottom, and three track subsections leave from the top. Note that the wires are strain-relieved by wire clamps to prevent damage to the joint with the circuit breaker should a wire get an accidental tug.

6 Here are several different types of track detectors. Either the track subsection bus is fed through the detector or it's passed through a large inductor. The track detector reports its status either through a digital signal on the connector or through the cab bus.

7

Bob Perrin has his track subsection equipment mounted to shelves under his layout. The power district transformer and booster are in the back. The Digitrax PM42 circuit breaker is in the front. The booster feeds the PM42 which in turn separates into four track subdistricts.

a moment to figure out that it was an operator around the corner that caused the short. On some systems, the booster emits an audible alarm that a short has occurred. This at least provides a clue about what went wrong, but it doesn't tell you who caused the short.

Short-circuits can sometimes be hard to trace. Along with trains, they can be caused by a stray strand of wire, a piece of debris (for example, a metal uncoupling pin that's fallen off a car), bare wires brushing into each other, or a faulty connector or switch.

By dividing each power district into subsections or subdistricts, potential problems are greatly reduced. Gaps cut into each rail and in the track bus are required.

The simplest method is to wire a toggle switch between the booster and each subsection's track bus. This doesn't provide automatic protection in case of a derailment, but it will make it easier to trace a pesky short-circuit on the layout.

The best method is a separate circuit breaker. Several companies make external circuit breakers designed specifically for DCC that can be used to isolate track

subsections. Some have multiple features including adjustable trip time and trip current. Some also include auto-reversers (see Chapter 4), track occupancy detection, and feedback to a computer via the cab bus. Just like the boosters themselves, the circuit breakers must be wired in-phase.

If you plan to install a signal system or otherwise add block occupancy detection, you can use any of several current-based block detectors designed specifically for DCC. In order for them to detect only a particular section of track you must further subdivide your track subsections into detection blocks. Separate circuit breakers aren't needed for each detection block, but you do have to make sure that all the power going to the rails in a detection block goes through the block detector. Most detector manufacturers recommend that each detector be connected as close to the track as possible to prevent false indications.

Like circuit breakers, there are a lot of choices for block detection. Many DCC system manufacturers produce them, and companies that make signal systems offer them as well.

Detectors have many features that can be customized by jumper wires or configuration variables. There are basically two ways that current is detected. One is by running a loop of wire (which goes to the track) through an inductor on the block detector. The second way is by routing the track power through the detector itself. In either case, all the track power that goes to that detection block must go through the block detector. Track feeders cannot bypass the block detector.

Block detectors have to feed their information back to whatever device is using the information. That can be a signal system, a dispatcher's panel, or a grade-crossing circuit. For those applications that use the DCC system or a computer connected to the DCC system, there are interfaces designed to connect your block detectors to your cab bus. These are highly specialized per DCC manufacturer.

A number of companies produce computer programs that can gather information from the block detectors, process it, and send information back out to wayside signals.

CHAPTER FOUR

Turnouts and reversing sections

Wiring turnouts for DCC isn't difficult, but does require some special attention and consideration.

Turnouts can require special care and wiring to operate (or to operate more reliably) with DCC. Also, as with any standard DC layout, you also need to be aware of reversing sections—such as reverse loops, wyes, and turntables—as all require rail gaps to avoid short circuits.

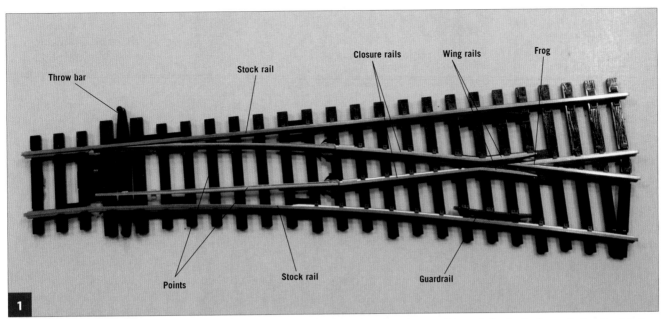

1 This Peco Electrofrog turnout is an example of a live-frog (power-routing) switch. On this type of turnout, the back of an out-of-gauge metal wheel can cause a short between the open point and the stock rail.

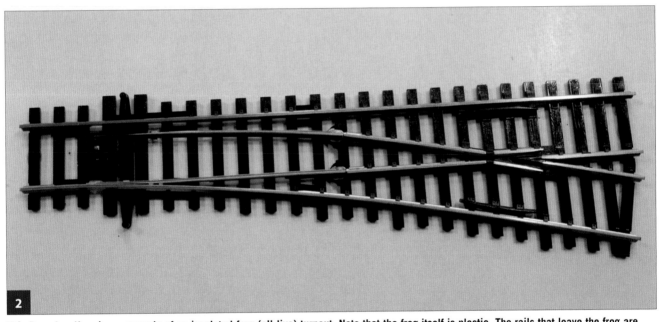

2 This Peco Insulfrog is an example of an insulated-frog (all-live) turnout. Note that the frog itself is plastic. The rails that leave the frog are opposite polarity. If the tread of a metal wheel is too wide, it can bridge the gap and cause a brief short circuit.

Turnouts and DCC

You may have heard that you need special turnouts to run DCC. That's not true, but you do have to pay some attention to turnout wiring.

You might discover that locomotives stutter, stall, or cause short circuits at turnouts on your DCC layout when they didn't have problems when the layout was powered by standard DC. This is due to momentary short circuits caused by locomotive wheels (or metal wheels of rolling stock) bridging rails

of opposite polarity as they pass over the turnout.

Because boosters supply much more current than a conventional DC power pack, they are equipped with fast-acting circuit breakers to protect the layout wiring and your models in the event of a short circuit. The circuit breaker automatically resets when tripped, but waits a period of time before it does. Most DC power packs are either not equipped with circuit breakers or they act slowly, so they don't trip when a

locomotive causes a momentary short and the locomotive's momentum carries it beyond the location of the short. It's not that the short circuit didn't occur with DC power, it's just that it wasn't as noticeable.

So what causes the short circuits? It depends on the type of turnout.

Turnouts fall into two categories: those with live frogs (sometimes called power-routing turnouts) and those with insulated frogs (also known as all-live turnouts). On a live-frog turnout, the frog is powered through the entire selected route. Old Shinohara, Peco Electrofrog, and Micro Engineering turnouts are examples of live-frog turnouts.

On an insulated-frog turnout, the point of the frog has no power or is "dead." Atlas, Kato Unitrack, Peco Insulfrog, and the new DCC-friendly Walthers turnouts fall into this category.

There are a couple of places that short circuits can occur in turnouts. On insulated-frog turnouts, the diverging rails leaving the frog can be close enough together that a wide-tread wheel can briefly bridge the two rails, which are of opposite polarity, **A**. Painting the railheads in this area with clear nail polish or enamel paint will help this problem, but will eventually need to be reapplied. Epoxy lasts a little longer.

Another potential source of a short circuit is between the points and the stock rail on a power-routing turnout, **B**. These turnouts count on the points to carry power to the frog. With out-of-gauge wheelsets or points, the back of a wheel can contact the point when it is away from the stock rail, causing a short.

This can be cured a couple of different ways. The first and most important thing is to make sure all wheelsets are in gauge. This not only reduces the likelihood of short circuits, but also prevents derailments. The second method is to wire the points to the adjacent stock rail so the two are always the same polarity. See the drawing below. This requires gaps in the closure rails near the frog, but then the frog isn't powered.

To make the frog "live" again, it must be wired to whichever stock rail is being contacted by the point when the turnout is lined in that direction. This can be done through auxiliary contacts on a switch machine or a separate switch that is thrown when the turnout is lined. Wiring the turnout as **C** shows will go a long way toward preventing short circuits.

Atlas Custom Line turnouts have a cast frog that can be made "live" by installing a switch and wiring to a tab built into the turnout.

Stationary decoders

Digital Command Control offers

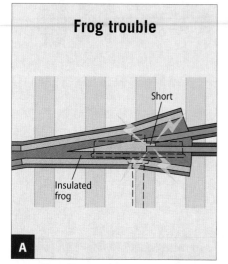

Frog trouble

A

Wide-profile metal wheels can bridge the two rails emerging from the insulated frog on some turnouts.

Point rails

B

A metal wheelset can briefly bridge the gap between the stock and point rails on a live-frog turnout, causing a short circuit.

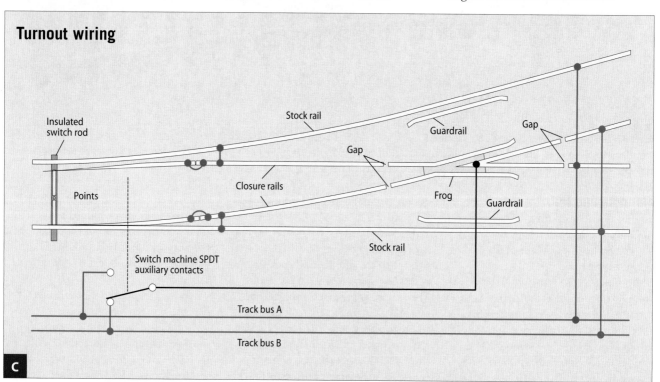

Turnout wiring

C

Wiring a power-routing (live-frog) turnout to isolate the points will eliminate point-to-stock short circuits.

remote control of switch-machine-equipped turnouts through a stationary or accessory decoder. These decoders are mounted on the layout and control accessories like turnouts and signals, along with just about any other device your imagination can come up with.

Stationary decoders can be controlled through your DCC throttle just like a locomotive decoder, but with a special set of commands. Some basic throttles and DCC systems can't issue stationary decoder commands, so if this is a feature you would like, consider it when choosing a DCC system. Stationary decoders from any manufacturer can be operated from any DCC system that supports stationary decoder commands.

Because stationary decoders come with varying features, choosing one can be complicated. Many are designed for turnouts, but they can often be adapted for other uses. For instance, I used a stationary decoder to control a friend's bascule bridge.

There are three types of switch machines that can be paired with stationary decoders. The first is the slow-motion stall machine. These have a small DC motor that is geared to move the turnout points at a very slow pace. They draw very little current and are always powered. Switchmaster and Tortoise are two examples.

The second type is the bi-polar machine, used on LGB and Kato turnouts. These machines require a little more kick than slow-motion machines and only draw power while actually moving the turnout points.

The third type is the twin-coil switch machine, including N.J. International and Atlas. These require a high current pulse to align the points, snapping them into place with a momentary pulse of power.

Some decoders can operate only one type of turnout machine, while others can control two or three types. Just like mobile decoders, stationary decoders use configuration variables (CVs) to control how they behave. Decoders that can control more than one type of switch machine rely on CVs to select the proper mode. Other CVs fine-tune the control by varying the width of the output pulses.

3 This locomotive has just caused a short circuit by running into an open turnout—note that the points are thrown for the other route. This is the most common cause of short circuits.

4 Derailments—especially at turnouts and crossings—can cause short circuits when the involved cars have metal wheels, as on these N scale hoppers.

5 Stationary decoders allow operators to control turnouts with their throttles. Both the switch machine and decoder are mounted below the layout.

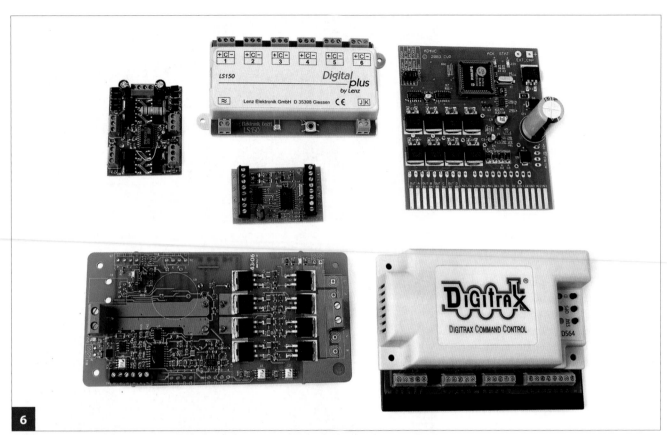

6

Stationary decoders include (clockwise from lower right) the Digitrax DS64, DCC Specialties PSX-ARFB, NCE Switch It, MRC 1628, Lenz LS150, and CVP Products AD4HC. Many stationary decoders are designed to power more than one switch machine.

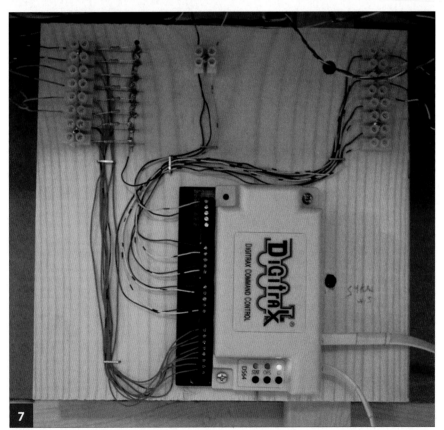

7

Bob Perrin mounts stationary decoders on panels under his layout. This is a Digitrax DS64 decoder, which can operate four switch machines.

Stationary decoders may be powered either by the DCC track bus or from a separate power supply. If the track bus is used, the wiring is already in place under the layout, but the amount of current it takes must be included when figuring out if you need multiple boosters. For stationary decoders that power slow-motion stall-type turnout machines, the current draw of all the turnout motors must also be included.

Loops, wyes, and turntables

DCC, like DC, has a polarity. At any given moment, one rail is more positive than the other. Track configurations like balloon tracks (reverse or return loops) and wyes cause track to turn back on itself, which results in a short circuit if not wired properly. This is true for both DC and DCC layouts.

Turntables are slightly different, as the rails themselves don't cause a short circuit, but a locomotive crossing from the turntable to an adjoining track will if they are not in phase.

Identifying reversing sections can sometimes be tricky. The bottom line is that if locomotive can start with the

8

NCE's Switch It stationary decoder powers two turnout motors. It's small enough to be attached directly to a Tortoise motor with double-sided foam tape.

engineer's side over the north rail and travel so that it is eventually positioned so that the engineer's side is over the south rail, you have a reversing section.

Reverse loops have a turnout feeding a loop of track, **D**. A double-track dog-bone layout can form an unintentional reverse loop: If one track of the double track loops around to the other track and there's a crossover between the two tracks, there is a reverse loop.

Techniques for wiring reversing sections for a DC layout will work just fine on a DCC layout, provided that the switch contacts are rated high enough for DCC booster current.

The traditional method for wiring a reverse loop is to isolate the reversing section from the rest of the layout, usually by the turnout. The reversing section must be longer than your longest train. The track in that section is wired with a double-pole double-throw (DPDT) toggle switch, shown in **D**. When operated with DCC, the DPDT switch can be thrown when the train is in the isolated section and the turnout lined in the opposite direction so the train would continue out of the reversing section. Since DCC does't use track polarity to determine locomotive direction, the train needn't stop and the direction on the throttle doesn't have to be changed.

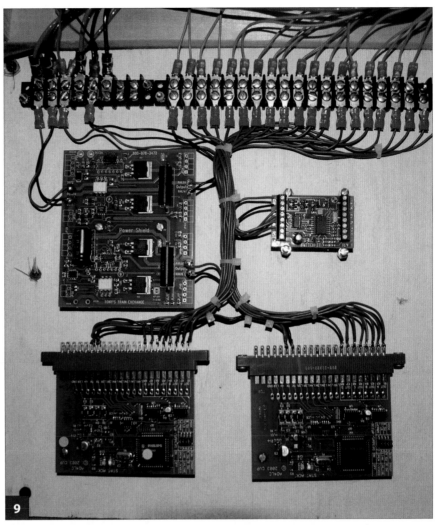

9

This panel under my layout contains stationary decoders to power the turnouts in a subdivision staging yard. The panel also contains a dual DCC track circuit breaker. One output is dedicated entirely for the stationary decoders.

10

Here's the wiring under my turntable. The green circuit board is the auto-reverser.

The DPDT switch can be the auxiliary contacts of a switch machine. This way, simply lining the turnout throws the switch as well.

A neat little gadget called an auto-reverser can be used to automatically control the polarity. An auto-reverser depends on the short circuit caused by the wheels crossing the isolation gap between the reversing section and other sections of track. They instantaneously reverse the polarity of the reversing section so that the short no longer occurs. This happens so quickly that no interruption of power to the locomotive is noticed.

Since DCC boosters and circuit breakers also trip when a short occurs, the auto-reverser must switch the polarity before the boosters and/or circuit breaker can trip. This can cause a problem as not all auto-reversers are compatible with all boosters/circuit breakers. Many auto-reversers and circuit breakers can be adjusted either by configuration variables or by jumpers or potentiometers. Even with all the adjustments, not all auto-reversers will work with all circuit breakers.

There are boosters and circuit breakers that have auto-reversers built into them but if you use that feature, you have to dedicate that booster/circuit breaker to the reversing section and have others for the rest of the layout.

The ways of wyes

Wyes also form a reversing section and there are a couple of traditional ways to wire the reversing section in a wye. If the tail of the wye is a stub (meaning it just ends and doesn't connect to any other track on the layout), the turnout at the tail can be wired so that the turnout and tail track is the reversing section. If the turnout has auxiliary electrical contacts, it can be wired to reverse polarity when the turnout is lined.

If the tail of the wye connects to the rest of the layout, one leg of the wye will have to be made the reversing section. If you use metal wheels or have lighted cars, the leg must be longer than your longest train. If not, it just has to be longer than your longest locomotive consist. A double-pole, double-throw switch can be wired to reverse the polarity of the wye

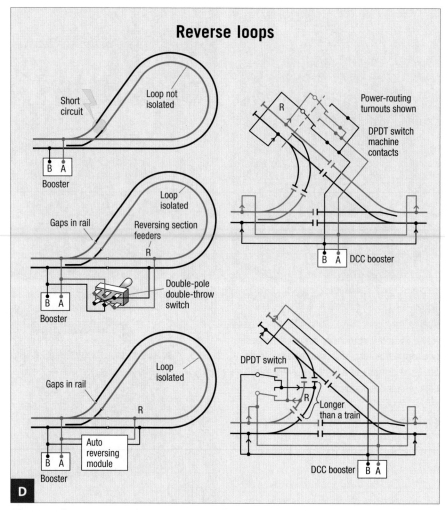

All reverse loops, wyes, and return tracks require special wiring to avoid short circuits.

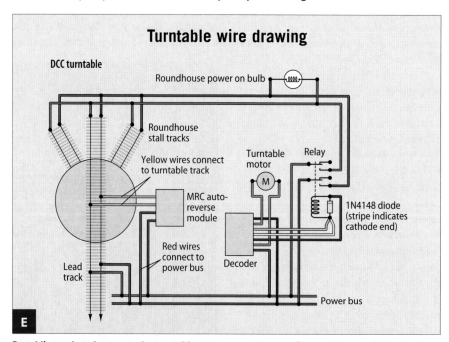

By adding a decoder to run the turntable motor, an auto-reversing module to switch polarity on the rails, and a relay to use the decoder's headlight function as an on/off switch, you can control all funcions of your turntable and roundhouse/storage tracks from your DCC cab, eliminating the need for a control panel.

11

It's relatively simple to wire a turntable so it can be controlled from a DCC cab.

leg just like a balloon track. DCC auto-reversers can also be used for wyes.

Turntables

Like wyes and balloon tracks, turntables also reverse your locomotives. Not all turntables are created equal though. Some commercial turntables have built-in reversers in the form of a split ring that automatically reverses polarity as the bridge rotates. Nothing special has to be done with that type of turntable so that it can operate on DCC, but if you operate sound decoders, you may find the sounds stop and restart as the turntable reverses polarity.

If you have a turntable that doesn't auto-reverse, you can wire its track to a DPDT toggle switch and throw the switch as the bridge rotates, however, it might be difficult to remember when to

throw the switch. The bridge polarity must always be such that the top rail is connected to the red polarity and the bottom rail to the black polarity.

A better way is to use a DCC auto-reverser, **E**. That way no switch is required and your operators don't have to be trained. Operation on and off the bridge is seamless.

I inherited my scratchbuilt Stevens Point roundhouse and turntable from my friend John Proebsting (*Great Model Railroads* 2002) when John passed away. John had a neat way to power the turntable. He used a bicycle hub for the bridge main bearing and powered one rail through that. The other rail was powered via the gallows using a dress snap as the pivoting contact. This method however does not auto-

reverse. As explained in my book *DCC Projects and Applications Volume 1,* I used an MRC auto-reverser to reverse the polarity and a mobile decoder to power the turntable motor. This worked fine until I decided to create a power district subsection of the track bus for the roundhouse and surrounding engine terminal. I discovered that the NCE EB3 circuit breaker I used tripped before the MRC auto-reverser could reverse. There are a number of circuit breakers with auto-reversers built in, but I didn't want to dedicate an entire power district subsection for the turntable bridge. I already had the turntable and power district wired so I simply substituted a DCC Specialties OG-AR auto-reverser for the MRC auto-reverser and everything worked as before.

CHAPTER FIVE

Cab bus wiring

Having a cab bus with multiple socket panels around your layout allows you to plug in throttles and other accessories at any convenient location.

Most DCC systems, especially the larger ones, allow for walkaround control. Standard throttles are tethered to the layout and can be moved from location to location by a series of jacks (plug-in sockets) along the fascia of the layout. The cable that connects the command station to the jacks is called a cab bus. Some DCC systems also have a control bus that connects system components such as boosters.

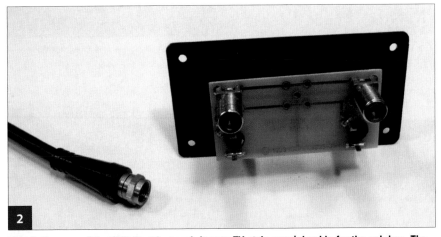

1

Throttle panels clockwise from upper left include a Digitrax radio panel with six-pin RJ tether port, an Easy DCC panel with two ¼" audio jacks, an Atlas (Lenz) panel with two DIN sockets and a six-pin RJ jack, and an NCE universal panel with two four-pin RJ jacks.

Tethered throttles have "memory"—that is, the system recalls the throttle settings when the throttle is unplugged from a socket, giving the operator time to plug the throttle back into another socket farther down the line.

Wireless throttles, using radio or infrared control, have become more popular in recent years. Even if you have radio-controlled throttles, chances are you'll have a tethered throttle or two as well. Further, many radio and infrared receivers interface to the command station via the cab bus.

Each DCC system employs a different style of cab bus, but all use readily available cables designed for other purposes. For instance, Digitrax, Lenz and NCE use a cable similar to the type used in some phone systems. MRC uses an eight-conductor cable commonly used for computer networks and CVP (Easy DCC) uses coaxial cable made for video systems.

Most DCC companies sell throttle panels designed to mount to the layout fascia. These house the cab jacks, with panels typically including two or more cab jacks on the front and at least two cab bus jacks on the rear. The cab bus provides a

2

This is the rear of the CVP throttle panel. It uses TV style coaxial cable for the cab bus. The other side has two jacks for the throttles' ¼" phone plugs.

connection from the command station to the first panel, and then from panel to panel in what is called a "daisy chain." The cab bus goes in one of the cab bus jacks in the rear and out the other. Some manufacturers allow the cab bus to split off from the daisy chain by dividing the bus in the chain and causing a stub, or tee.

Phone cable cab buses

Typical modern phone systems employ module connectors called RJs (registered

jacks). For DCC cab buses there are basically three types. The first is a six-conductor type that uses six-conductor cable and RJ connectors that have six places and six conductors (6P6C). The second is a four-conductor type that has six places and four conductors (6P4C). Because both styles have six places, it is possible to plug a six-conductor plug into a four-position jack and vice-versa. This can come in very handy, because in some six-conductor buses the outer two wires

3 Phone cables can be made in two different ways. Note that with the cable flat, the plastic tabs on the connectors are both "up." This indicates pin 1 is connected to pin 6. This style of cable is not generally used.

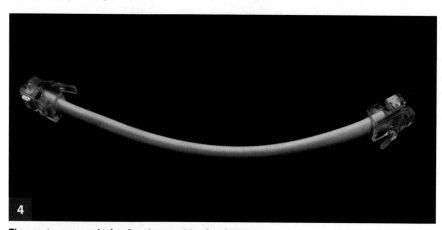

4 The most common design for phone cables is with one tab pointing up and the other down. This connects pin 1 of one connector to pin 1 of the other connector. This is how most DCC cab bus cables should be wired.

5 Here's a standard Digitrax throttle panel, with two jacks, installed on the fascia of Bob Perrin's HO scale Illinois Central layout.

are optional, allowing the use of four-conductor plugs as throttle jacks in some locations.

The third type is an eight-position RJ45 which has a larger connector than the first two. At first glance it looks like a phone cable, but it is wider. This type of cable and connector is commonly used for computer networks.

Phone cable buses (Digitrax, Lenz and NCE) have panel jacks that are quite similar; in fact, Tony's Train Exchange sells a universal panel jack that can be used for any of the three systems.

Phone cable with connectors at each end can be purchased in many lengths. You can also make your own cables to the exact lengths needed for your layout. To do this, you'll need the cable, connectors, and a crimper. All of these can be purchased at a local hardware or electronics store (such as Radio Shack). If you do this, I recommend buying a high-quality crimper—it just might save hours debugging a bad connection caused by a cheap crimper.

The cables can be made in two ways. The most common way is to connect pin 1 of the connector at one end of the cable to pin 1 at the other end of the cable. This requires the tab of the connector to be "up" on one end and "down" on the other. The other way is to connect pin 1 to pin 6 (or on four-conductor cable pin 1 to pin 4). This configuration occurs when both tabs are "up."

Care must be taken with extremely long buses as throttles that are plugged in sometimes draw their power from the bus. Just like with the track bus, the smaller the wire used in the cab bus, the larger the voltage drop and thus the increased likelihood of unpredictable operation if the voltage drop is too much. It's not always easy to determine the gauge of the wire in the cable before you buy it as it is sometimes not listed on the packaging. If you do experience trouble with your throttles because they are underpowered, most throttle panels have power jacks built in that allow you to plug an external power supply (usually a plug-in "wall-wart" type) into the bus to boost the power along the way.

Try to limit the length of a run where the cab bus and track bus run parallel in close proximity. If possible, separate them by at least 12". It's OK if they cross each other at angles around 90 degrees.

The following information on how to wire various DCC manufacturers' cab buses are meant a guide—always check the manual for your system. Along with the manual for the system itself, I've found the manuals for the throttle plates to contain some very useful information about wiring buses.

Digitrax LocoNet

Digitrax calls its cab bus LocoNet, and it also serves as the system's control bus because it connects boosters and other accessories to the command station. There are very few restrictions on wiring LocoNet. It may contain stubs but should not be looped back upon itself. Digitrax's throttle panels also contain an LED that can be wired to a section of nearby track to indicate whether it is powered or not.

Digitrax throttles contain batteries, so they don't draw their power from the bus, but the batteries can be drained when the DCC system is not powered. To prevent that, the throttle panel also has small connector for plugging in a power supply. This powers the cab bus when the command station is off and keeps the batteries on any throttles plugged into the throttle panels from going dead between operating sessions.

The main connector on LocoNet has pin-out shown in the chart on page 39. The colors indicated are those of a standard phone cable. Pins 1 and 6 are the same signal, Rail Sync. Pins 2 and 5 are both ground, and pins 3 and 4 are both LocoNet. This means that within a cable, pin 1 can be connected to pin 1 or pin 6—it makes no difference. Therefore the cables can be made with both sides "up" or one "up" and one "down" and the cab bus still functions. I still recommend making all the cables the same way, however. It's always best to keep things simple, which might help troubleshooting a problem later.

Digitrax designed LocoNet not only as a cab bus but also as the main communication bus of the system. The Digitrax signal system, additional boosters, and computer interfaces are connected to LocoNet and can report information back to the command station

6

Throttle panels, like this universal one from Tony's Train Exchange, connect to the cab bus. In this case, the black cable on the left goes to the command station and the white cable on the right goes to the next throttle panel along the fascia. Additional throttle panels are connected in daisy-chain fashion. A small layout might only require one or two throttle panels.

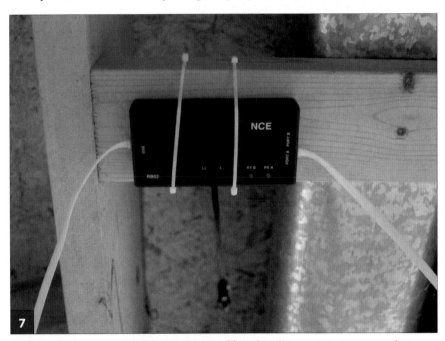

7

Radio transceivers—such as this one on the ceiling of my layout room—are among the accessories that can be plugged into a cab bus. The cable on the left is the cab bus; the cable on the right connects NCE radio transceivers to the radio repeaters.

or to a computer connected to LocoNet.

Digitrax's infrared and radio receivers for wireless throttles are built into specialized throttle panels. Digitrax also sells a tester, the LT1, for testing the bus cables once they are made.

Lenz XpressNet

Lenz calls its cab bus XpressNet, and it uses a four-conductor cable. Several other DCC system manufacturers use XpressNet as well, including Atlas, Hornby, Roco, and ZTC. Lenz

8

At the end of my cab bus, I use a commercial phone jack as a throttle panel rather than one specifically made for DCC. Only one plug-in is needed here.

9

The cable is simply wired to the rear of the phone jack. On the NCE cab bus, the outer two wires are reserved for future use, so I was able to use a four-conductor jack.

XpressNet can be split off to form tees by using commercial four- or six-conductor phone splitters (be careful when shopping, because some commercial splitters have only two conductors). The bus may not loop back upon itself, but according to Lenz it can be up to 3,000 feet long!.

An external 12-volt power source can be connected to pins 5 and 2 (L and M) to supply power if more than a few throttles are plugged into the bus.

You are by no means limited to using phone cable for the bus. If you are using five-pin DIN connectors, you may choose to wire individual jacks into the fascia of your layout and solder larger-gauge twisted-pair wire, such as bell wire, to connect them. The RS-485 lines (B and A) should be twisted together. Always make sure you connect the same wires to the same pins of the DIN connector. Consult the Lenz manual for the wiring of DIN connectors.

The end of the bus requires a 120-ohm resistor, which Lenz supplies with the system.

Wiring the NCE cab bus

The NCE cab bus also uses six-conductor phone cable. Its throttle panels have two jacks in the back and two in the front, all wired together. The two in the back are to daisy-chain the cab bus cables from panel to panel, and the jacks in the front are for throttles. The pin-out of the jacks is shown in the chart on page 39.

The electrical technology (a standard called RS-485) is the same as the Lenz system, so the same rules apply. Commercial phone splitters can be used to tee the bus, but don't loop it back on itself. In the strictest sense, four-conductor cable could be used for the NCE cab bus, but NCE has reserved pins 1 and 6 for future use, so using four-conductor cable might keep you from taking advantage of features NCE adds in the future.

Even though Lenz and NCE use the same RS-485 electrical standard, the throttles are not interchangeable. The data sent over wires is different; in other words, they speak a different language.

NCE's radio throttles can either be plugged into the bus or operate via radio. The radio transceiver, however, must be

throttles use either a five-pin circular connector, sometimes called a DIN, or a four-conductor RJ phone connector. The Lenz throttle panel has both styles of connectors on the front and a six-conductor jack on the back. The extra two wires are for a control bus

connection for operation of older-type Lenz command stations via the LH200 Master cab.

Because the pin-out is not a mirror of itself like Digitrax, the cables must be made with pin 1 connecting to pin 1 (one tab "up" and one tab "down").

plugged into the cab bus. NCE's radio system has optional radio repeaters that can be placed around the layout room. However, the radio repeaters are not connected to the cab bus, but rather are connected to the transceiver by a four-wire phone cable.

Like Lenz, NCE offers throttle panels with an optional five-pin DIN connector for the throttle side of the panel. The back of the panel still has RJ jacks.

NCE's radio throttles use batteries, and those are only used for power when the throttle is operating in radio mode. When any throttle is plugged into the cab bus, it draws its power from pins 2 and 5. Because of phone wire's typically small size, NCE recommends that any bus over 30 feet long have an additional 12-volt power supply added every 30 feet. The current provided by these power supplies must be enough to power all the throttles that could be on the bus at the same time. Each ProCab throttle draws about 120 mA, and the smaller throttles draw less current. Other accessories you may have on the bus, like fast clocks or NCE's mini-panel, also draw current that have to be accounted for.

CVP's Easy DCC cab bus

Easy DCC's cab bus consists of coaxial (coax) cable like the kind commonly used for TV connections. There must be a connection between the command station and an external board called the Throttle Extender. This connection is made by a six-pin phone cable, like that required for Digitrax, Lenz and NCE, and cannot be more than seven feet long. The cable must have both tabs "up" as described earlier. The Throttle Extender requires its own power supply in the form of a 12-volt AC, 1.5-amp plug-in pack.

From the Throttle Extender, coax cable connects the throttle panels in daisy-chain fashion. Do not use commercial TV coax splitters to create tees—instead add more Throttle Extenders. At the end of the cab bus, a 75-ohm, three-watt termination resistor is required.

Additional Throttle Extenders are connected daisy-chain style via six-conductor phone cable. The total length of all the six-conductor cables can't exceed seven feet, so all Throttle

I used a commercial six-conductor phone cable splitter to "tee" the cab bus right at the command station.

A: Pin-connection references					
Pin no.	Wire Color	NCE Cab Bus	Digitrax LocoNet	Lenz Xpress Net	Lenz DIN 5
1	White	No connection (Reserved)	Rail Sync	No connection	"C"
2	Black	Ground	Ground	Ground	"M"
3	Red	- RS-485	LocoNet	-RS-485	"B"
4	Green	+ RS-485	LocoNet	+RS-485	"A"
5	Yellow	+12 volts	Ground	+12 Volts	"L"
6	Blue	No connection (Reserved)	Rail Sync	No connection	"D"

Extenders must be located near the command station.

The Easy DCC manual is well-written and covers cab bus wiring in great detail.

MRC's cab bus

MRC's Prodigy Advance, Express, and Advance 2 rely on eight-conductor modular connectors (commonly called RJ-45) for the cab bus, making use of computer data cables.

The command station includes three jacks for plugging in throttles. If you

require more jacks, MRC sells throttle panels. Cables can be daisy-chained from throttle panel to throttle panel, and they can also be teed by either using a splitter (MRC offers them, or you can make your own). The command station supplies enough power for six throttles. If you require more than that, you'll need a special throttle panel with a power supply.

Like the Digitrax bus, the pin-out is a mirror of itself so it doesn't matter if the cables are made pin 1 to pin 1 or pin 1 to pin 8.

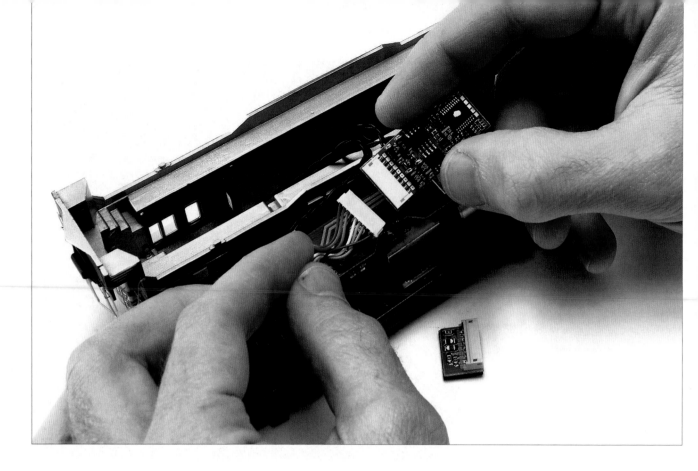

CHAPTER SIX

Decoder installation and programming

Many decoder installations are as easy as slipping a decoder plug into a socket on the locomotive. This is a Lenz LE1014-JST decoder with a nine-pin JST plug being installed in an HO scale Athearn Ready-To-Roll locomotive.

Once your layout is wired and your DCC system is installed, the last thing you'll need before you can operate is at least one locomotive equipped with a DCC decoder. This chapter will explain how to install different types of decoders, how to program them, and how to set up multiple locomotives to run together in consists.

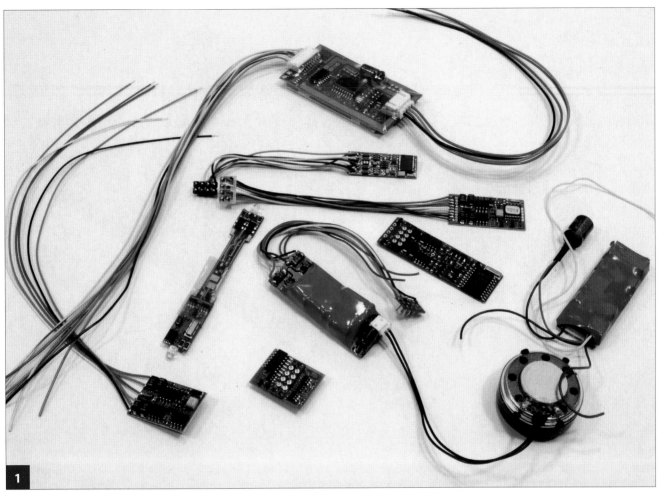

A wide variety of decoders is available, including drop-in, plug-equipped, and hard-wired models.

Decoders come in all sizes and styles, **1**. It's possible to find a decoder for just about any locomotive. There are decoders designed as drop-in replacements for specific locomotives, and there are also generic decoders that can be hard-wired (soldered) into many different types of locomotives. Also, more and more locomotives are now available from the factory with standard or sound-equipped decoders already installed. Let's go through the installation steps on a few different locomotives.

Drop-in replacements

The easiest type of decoder to install is a drop-in circuit board. I chose an MRC sound decoder designed for the N scale Athearn FP45, **2**. This sound decoder has the speaker built into the circuit board, **3**, so it's completely self-contained.

The toughest thing about this installation is removing the locomotive shell, which really isn't that difficult. Like most diesel locomotive models

these days, removing the shell requires taking off the couplers. After that, gentle upward pressure on the pilot pops the shell off.

Slide the original light board forward and out. Place the new decoder in and slide it to the back, **4**. Replace the shell and you're done!

My first recommendation for any decoder installation is to test it on your programming track before trying to run it on your layout. Your programming track has a limited amount of current, so if something is wired improperly or a short circuit is occurring, it is less likely that the decoder will be damaged on the programming track.

A quick test of a decoder installation is to simply read back CV1 with your DCC system. The read-back process will check the motor and rail connections. If you are successful, CV1's value will be 3—all new decoders are shipped from the factory with the short address (CV1) programmed as a 3. This is a good

time to program a new address into the decoder since every locomotive must have a unique address. The locomotive number is almost always a good choice as an address.

The lighting and sound must be tested on the main line, but by checking the rail and motor wiring on the programming track, you're less likely to have a wiring problem that will damage your decoder.

Another easy decoder installation is the Proto 2000 GP30, **5**, which has an eight-pin, dual-in-line socket. The NMRA has defined the size and pin-out of this socket as a recommended practice (RP), and most model manufacturers and decoder companies follow this standard.

Proto 2000 has a unique installation of the socket, which is attached by wires to the locomotive rather than built into the light board. These wires go to the motor, wheels, and lights. The locomotive's light board has an 8-pin plug that mates with the socket.

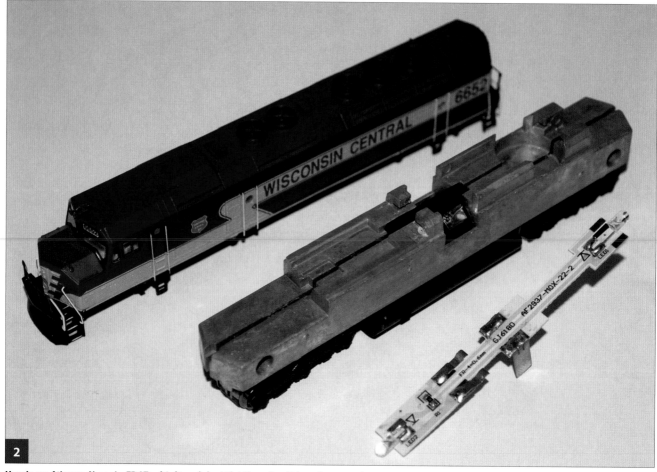

2 Here's an Athearn N scale FP45 with its original lighting-circuit board removed.

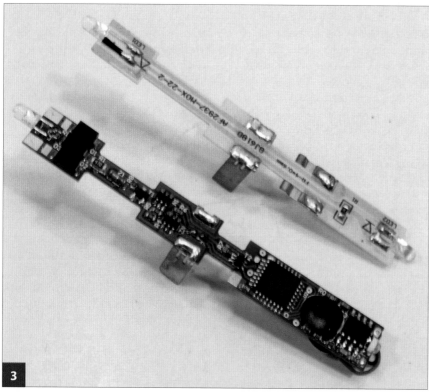

3 MRC's drop-in sound decoder for the N scale Athearn FP45 is in the foreground, next to the model's original light board.

For this model I chose an NCE decoder (the P2K-SR), which is designed to replace the light board in many different Proto 2000 models.

Start by unplugging and removing the light board. The back of the decoder requires a piece of electrical tape to insulate it.

If you retain the original lights in the original light pipes, just attach the socket to the plug, reassemble the locomotive, and test it on your programming track. (See the following section on lighting for more details.)

Several models by Atlas, Athearn Genesis, Kato, and Stewart share a common style of light board, with four tabs at each end and two tabs in the middle. Wires from the locomotive attach to these tabs by plastic clips. Several manufacturers make drop-in decoders that replace these boards. The decoders vary in features and number of lighting functions.

To install a decoder in one of those locomotives, pull off the clips and the

4

The MRC sound decoder is an easy drop-in installation in the FP45.

light board, **6**. It's usually pretty easy to keep track of which wires go to which tabs, but make sure they all wind up on the same tabs of the decoder. I don't recommend reusing the plastic clips—solder the wires to ensure solid connections.

The outer two tabs on each end are connected to the rails, and the two tabs on the side in the middle are connected to the motor. The two center tabs on each end are for the front and rear headlights, except for F units, in which case the rear headlight tabs can be connected to a second headlight or classification light in front.

Be careful when connecting the lighting tabs. Some locomotives use low-voltage (1.5V) light bulbs, **7**, or LEDs. It is important to find out what voltage the bulbs are before connecting them to the decoder. The Athearn Genesis F3 shown uses 1.5V bulbs. An easy way to determine that is to connect the bulb to a AA battery. If it shines brightly, it is a 1.5 V bulb.

Some decoder lighting outputs (often called "function" outputs) are made for 12-14V bulbs. If this is the case for the decoder you are using, you'll need a dropping resistor—a resistor wired in series with the bulbs. I used an 820-ohm, ½-watt resistor for the Athearn model, **8**.

To calculate the value of the dropping resistor for a headlight, follow Ohm's Law: voltage = current x resistance (or resistance = voltage/current. The voltage for the formula is the voltage needed to drop across the resistor. Usually this is approximately the DCC track voltage minus 1V.

The current in the formula is the current of the light bulb. This can vary from 10 mA to 100 mA, but it's hard to know for sure without measuring it, so I usually just start with a 1K-ohm resistor and gradually reduce the value until the bulb is burning at the correct intensity.

To calculate the power rating required for the resistor, multiply the resistor voltage by the bulb current. You can always use a higher wattage resistor,

but don't use a smaller one. If you are just under the resistor's rating, it's likely to get hot, so be conservative and use the biggest resistor you have room for. Standard resistor power ratings are ⅛, ¼, ½, and 1 watt. The NCE decoder manual has a nifty chart that helps determine resistor values and ratings.

Hard-wired decoders

If a locomotive doesn't have a socket and no drop-in circuit-board replacement decoders are available, you'll have to hard-wire the decoder. You might also want to consider hard-wiring a decoder if there are particular features you're looking for, such as additional lighting functions, fine motor control, or sounds that aren't available in the drop-in decoders available for your locomotive.

I had an old Athearn F unit with a new motor (a Mashima can motor) in which I wanted a decoder installed, **9, 10**. This model had no lighting, but most—if not all—wired decoders have at least two lighting functions that I could have used.

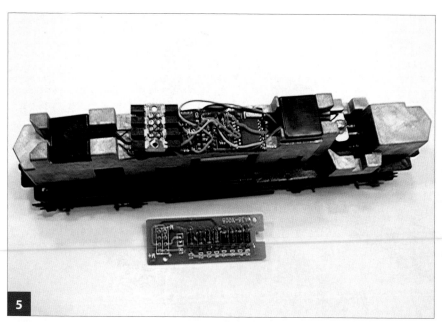

5 Several manufacturers offer decoders to fit Proto 2000 locomotives (this is an **NCE P2K-SR** in an older HO Proto 2000 GP30). The original light board is next to the locomotive.

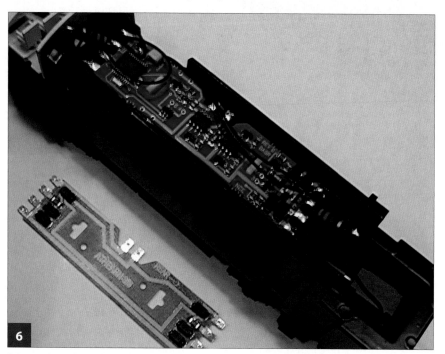

6 Athearn Genesis F units and others share a common type of light board, and several manufacturers offer drop-in replacement decoders. The old light board is on the left.

Thanks to the NMRA RP color coding, installing a wired decoder is pretty straightforward, but you must be aware of a few details.

Most importantly, the motor must be completely electrically isolated from the frame and wheels. Often in older locomotives, the frame carries power from one rail to the motor, which is mounted directly to the frame. If that is the case, the motor must be insulated from the locomotive frame. Remove the motor and mounting clip and re-install it using electrical tape to insulate it from the frame, and double-sided foam tape to hold it in place.

The motor's current rating must also be taken into account. The decoder must be rated above the amount of current the locomotive draws. Some older open-frame motors in HO locomotives would draw .5A to .75A or more; modern can motors generally draw less than .5A. In my case, the locomotive was repowered with a low-current can motor.

In this old Athearn, one of the rails was connected electrically to the frame. To get around this, I had to drill and tap a hole in the frame. I then installed a screw in the hole and soldered a wire to it, **11**.

Following the NMRA color code, the decoder's black and red wires are attached to the rails. The red wire is attached to the right rail as the locomotive is running forward (this is only crucial if you will be running a decoder-equipped engine on a conventional DC layout).

The orange and gray wires are attached to the motor. It can be difficult to determine the correct orientation of these wires, but never fear: No harm will occur if you reverse these. Your locomotive will simply run backward, which can be corrected in two ways. You can reverse the two wires. Or, if that is difficult to do (such as if you've replaced the shell and don't want to disassemble anything), you can change the "configuration" CV (CV29). By programming this CV properly, you can reverse the direction of your locomotive when the DCC throttle indicates it is travelling in the forward direction. Consult your decoder manual for the programming instructions for CV29.

If I had decided to add lighting, I would have used the function wires on the decoder. The blue wire is the lighting common. It is attached to one side of all your lights and is always on. It carries a positive voltage equal to the DCC track voltage minus about one volt.

The white wire is function 0, which is the forward headlight. It is switched on when function 0 is turned on with the DCC throttle and the locomotive is running forward.

If you are use low-voltage bulbs you'll have to use a dropping resistor as described earlier. If you are using an LED, a current limiting resistor must be used. Its value is calculated just like a voltage dropping resistor for light bulbs. The LED anode must be connected to the blue wire and the cathode to the current limiting resistor. The other side of the resistor is connected to the function wire.

The yellow wire is the rear headlight. This is usually controlled by function 0 as well, and is activated when the locomotive runs in reverse. Some decoders have additional lighting functions and wires.

In this installation, I wired the motor and rail wires, attached the decoder atop the motor with double-sided foam tape, and tied back the unused wires. I held it all in place with electrical tape, **12**.

Through the use of CVs, some decoders allow function wires to be controlled by other function buttons on the throttle. Also, a number of lighting effects such as strobe lights and ditch lights can be programmed.

Basic programming

Each decoder has a series of numbers programmed into it called configuration variables (CVs). A decoder's CVs determine how it will behave. Certain CVs, like the locomotive address, are essential for a locomotive to function on a DCC layout. Others, like momentum control, are optional. There are dozens of different CVs and they vary from decoder to decoder. Most decoders have only a fraction of the total possible CVs.

DCC systems use menus on their throttles or command station to both program and read back the CVs of a decoder while the locomotive is on the programming track, **13**. The command station sends low-power specialized DCC commands through the rails to a single locomotive. Only one locomotive should be on the programming track at one time.

To read back CVs, the command station plays a game of "20 Questions" with the decoder. The command station sends a command to the decoder asking if a CV has a particular value. The decoder responds "yes" by sending an electrical pulse to the locomotive's motor causing a temporary increase in the current. The command station is able to detect the increased current in the programming track and knows the answer to the question. For instance, if a locomotive's short address (CV1) is set to 02, the command station might ask "is CV1 a 1? The decoder would not respond. After a moment, the command station asks "is CV1 a 2?" This time

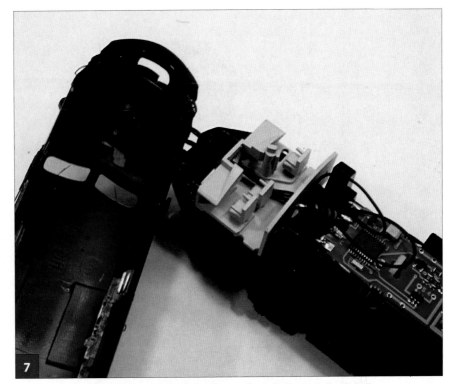

The front headlight and signal light of the Athearn Genesis Fs are 1.5-volt bulbs, so a voltage-dropping resistor must be wired in series with the bulb.

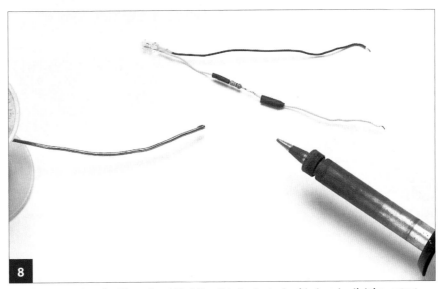

A resistor must be wired in series with 1.5-volt bulbs to work with decoder lighting output functions.

the motor would get a pulse from the decoder, and the command station would recognize it and know that CV1 is set to the number 2.

The specific steps and buttons used to program a decoder vary by system and throttle. See your system manual for details on the exact steps and process required.

Some configuration variables are simple to program—for example, the locomotive's address. Others are a little more complex—see page 49.

Consisting

The simplest way to run multiple units together with DCC is to program the decoders in each locomotive to the same address. This is most efficient with a permanently coupled set of locomotives, such as an A-B-A set of F units. For instance, I have a set of F3s numbered

9

This is an older HO Athearn standard locomotive that has been repowered with a can motor.

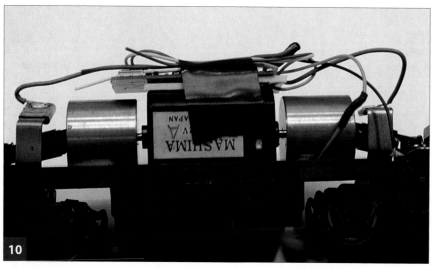

10

Electrical tape keeps the loose ends of the wires from contacting the flywheels.

2200A, 2200B, and 2200C. Since I use four-digit addressing on my layout, I like to have the decoder address match the unit's road number, so I have the 2200 part covered. The A, B, and C part is a bit of a problem because that's more than four digits.

I could assign the units decoder addresses 2201, 2202, and 2203, but I also have a locomotive numbered 2201B, so that won't work. And, I don't want these units to be exceptions to my rule of matching the decoder address to the road number, making it difficult for my operators to figure out how select these engines.

To solve my dilemma, I used a drawbar to permanently link the units

Just about every kind of light you see on a full-size locomotive can be duplicated on a model. In addition to front and rear headlights, prototype locomotives have numerous other lights. Modern diesels are equipped with ditch lights that can alternately flash when the horn is blown. Others have rooftop strobe lights. Diesels from earlier eras had oscillating signal lights (Mars lights) and rotating rooftop beacons. Platform lights, cab lights, and step lights have been features on diesels since their early days.

Lighting effects aren't just for diesels. Steam locomotives were almost always equipped with class lights and sometimes signal lights, and the tenders had marker lights.

Digital Command Control decoders power lighting effects through function outputs. These outputs are activated by the throttle's function buttons, and configuration variables (CVs) determine how these functions work.

The term "function" is sometimes confusing because it refers to both an actual wire (or terminal) on the decoder and the buttons on a throttle. Not all decoders have a full range of outputs. If you want three different lighting effects on a locomotive, you must use a decoder with at least three function outputs.

Each function output consists of a single wire or terminal. A common wire is used for all functions to complete the circuit. On most decoders, the blue wire is common, per National Model Railroad Association Recommended Practice 9.1.1. It's usually around +12-14 volts.

The function output is actually a ground connection when the function is on. Some newer decoders have a +5V common for use with low-voltage light bulbs and light-emitting diodes (LEDs). A smaller resistor is needed for these lights.

Ditch lights require two function outputs if you want them to flash alternately. The common wire is connected to both ditch lights and two function outputs are connected, one to each light.

Make sure you choose a decoder that can provide the lighting effects you want. Not all decoders let you program lighting effects on all of the function outputs, and some don't support any lighting effects.

A summary of each decoder's features is usually listed on its package, but I'd recommend reading the decoder manual first. Most manuals are available at the manufacturer's website.

To get a lighting function output to do something other than be on constantly, you must program CVs. The CV number and the CV value will vary between decoders. By programming the lighting effect CVs with different values, various effects can be achieved.

There is typically a CV for each function output. A list of values for each effect is in the decoder manual. In some cases, the flash rate or light intensity can be programmed.

Another thing to consider when choosing a decoder is the output current available on the function outputs. A single function output must be able to supply the current for all lights controlled by that function. Light bulbs can draw anywhere from 10mA to 100mA, and LEDs use between 5 and 20mA. Today's decoders can usually supply enough current for all but the biggest lighting jobs.

Most new locomotives use 1.5V bulbs. If the blue common wire is used, a resistor is needed to drop the 12-14V of the function output to 1.5V for the bulb. If the +5V common is used with a 1.5V bulb, you'll need a smaller dropping resistor. For more information on selecting resistors, see page 64 in my book *DCC Projects and Applications*, and consult the decoder manual.

LEDs require a current-limiting resistor. Resistor value can be calculated the same way as for a voltage-dropping resistor. The forward voltage of an LED is typically between 2 and 3V.

Because of the differences in characteristics between light bulbs and LEDs, different CV values may be needed when programming lighting effects. Some decoder manufacturers recommend not using LEDs at all.

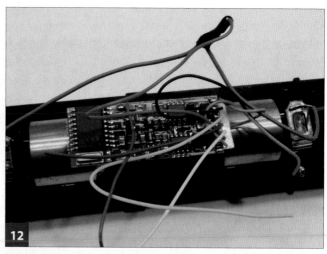

The frame of many older models, such as this Athearn, carries power from one of the rails. The original motor frame directly contacted the locomotive frame. When installing a DCC decoder, the motor must be isolated from the frame. The black wire is soldered to the head of a screw that has been mounted to the frame.

This view shows the decoder wired in place and attached to the top of the motor with double-sided foam tape.

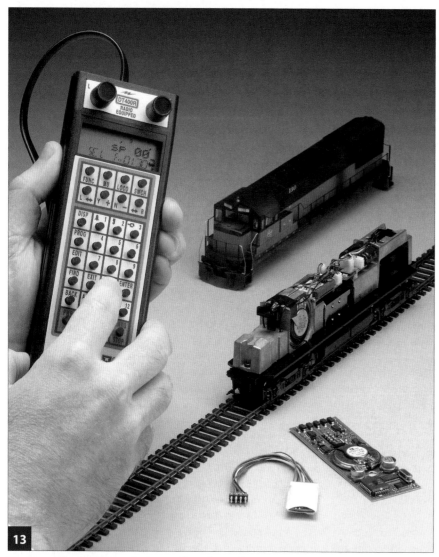

The locomotive address and other configuration variables are programmed to the decoder using a throttle (Digitrax in this case).

and assigned the three-unit consist the address 2200. The rear unit is facing the opposite direction, so I had to reverse its direction using CV29. Now all of the locomotives respond to the information packets addressed to 2200.

Controlling the headlights and Mars lights in the A units is still a problem. I don't like directional lighting because it isn't prototypical, but I made an exception in this case. I felt it was a good compromise, since the A-B-A set is rarely used for switching. When the 2200A is leading, its headlight is lit and the trailing 2200B's headlight is off. The lighting effect is opposite when 2200B is on the point.

I used F1 to control the Mars light on 2200A, and F2 to operate it on 2200B. I wrote this on the engine cards for the A-B-A set so operators know how to activate the Mars light.

Some DCC systems, such as Digitrax, use universal consisting as the primary method of consisting. Locomotives with different addresses can be controlled as one unit. In this method, the DCC system's command station keeps track of which units are in a consist.

Each manufacturer has a different method for universal consisting. On my NCE system, it's called old-style consisting. Despite the name, it has some advantages, especially for lighting effects. Since the command station keeps track of the consist, it sends the same speed

Mobile decoders used in locomotives and stationary decoders used to operate accessories can be customized using configuration variables (CVs). Think of a CV like a file folder with a piece of paper in it. With your DCC system, you can write a number on that piece of paper and put it back in the folder. The decoder can look at the number in the folder and act upon its value. Since there are many CVs, there are many different file folders in a single decoder.

Configuration variables range from the very simple (decoder address) to more complex (back-electromotive-force control). The CVs control a variety of features, from lighting effects to what style of horn is played by a sound decoder.

Not all maker's decoders have the same CVs, and even those that do often don't work in the same way. There are, however, several essential CVs designated by the National Model Railroad Association (NMRA) to operate the same way in all decoders.

One of those is CV1. This is the primary address, sometimes called the two-digit or short address. When the DCC system instructs a decoder what to do, it first sends an address through the rails so a specific decoder knows to listen for commands. The values for CV1 can be 0 to 127, but not all systems use the entire range. In some decoders, a value of 0 for CV1 takes the decoder out of DCC. Other DCC systems don't use addresses between 100-127, making it truly a two-digit address.

I find the range of 1-127 too limiting for my decoder addresses, so I make use of CVs 17 and 18, which are the extended address CVs, sometimes called the four-digit or long address. This lets me use the locomotive's three- or four-digit road number for the decoder address.

CVs 17 and 18 combine to create any number between 1 and 10,239, although many DCC systems limit that range. Some systems treat any address below 100 as a primary address, while others will not support addresses above 9,999. A few DCC systems won't recognize extended addresses at all.

Sounds complicated, doesn't it? Sometimes it is. Combining CV17 and CV18 to create a number for an address isn't always easy. Thankfully, most DCC systems take care of the math for you. With most systems, the fact that you're programming these CVs is completely transparent to the user. All you need to know is that you want to program the four-digit address.

Changing CVs

There are a few ways to change CVs. Most DCC systems have terminals on the command station for a programming track (see chapter 2). These are connected to a piece of track isolated from the rest of the layout. Mine is on my workbench, but you could use a siding as long as it's electrically isolated from the rest of the layout.

A locomotive on a programming track can have its CVs changed in service mode programming. Using the DCC throttle or a control panel, the CV can be modified or read back. Only one locomotive can be on the programming track at a time. Some sound decoders draw more current than some programming tracks can supply. SoundTraxx and DCC Specialties sell programming boosters to overcome that problem.

Certain decoders and DCC systems will also take advantage of operations (ops) mode programming, or programming on the main. This uses any track on your layout to program CVs. Any number of locomotives can be on the track at the same time.

Reading back CVs on the screen of your throttle is useful when you're experimenting with CV values like speed matching, ditch light flashing rate, or sound volume. However, CVs can't be read back in operations mode.

If programming CVs seems complicated, don't worry. Other than the locomotive address, you don't *have* to program any CVs. However, there are several ways to figure out how to program CVs. Many decoder manuals contain step-by-step instructions. Some DCC systems are very intuitive and walk you through the steps in plain English. In my opinion, the coolest method for programming CVs is with a computer.

There are several ways to connect your computer to your decoder. The first is through your DCC system. Many DCC systems have computer interfaces available. Software, such as the free DecoderPro (jmri.sourceforge.net), allow you to select decoder features with the click of a mouse. Model Rectifier Corp. also has decoder programming software. Visit www.modelrec.com for more information.

The second is through programming boxes such as Digitrax's PS3, QSI Solutions' Quantum Programmer, and ESU's LokSound Programmer. These were originally intended for programming sound decoders, but also allow you to program other CVs. Each is a small box that connects to either the USB or serial port of your computer and to your programming track. (Do not connect these boxes to your DCC system.)

Configuration variables may sound intimidating, but with a little patience and the aid of your DCC system or a computer, they can help you get the most out of your decoder.

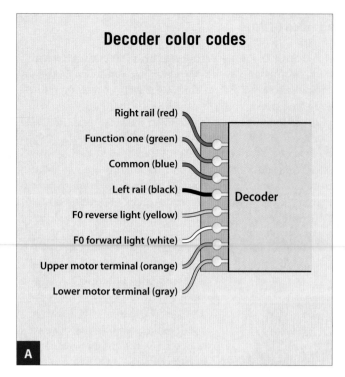

Decoder color codes

Right rail (red)
Function one (green)
Common (blue)
Left rail (black)
F0 reverse light (yellow)
F0 forward light (white)
Upper motor terminal (orange)
Lower motor terminal (gray)

Decoder

A

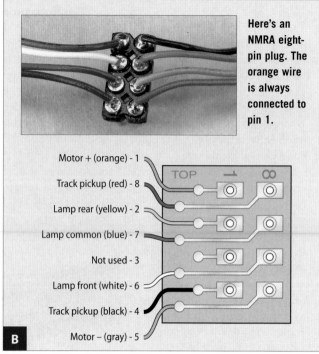

Here's an NMRA eight-pin plug. The orange wire is always connected to pin 1.

Motor + (orange) - 1
Track pickup (red) - 8
Lamp rear (yellow) - 2
Lamp common (blue) - 7
Not used - 3
Lamp front (white) - 6
Track pickup (black) - 4
Motor − (gray) - 5

TOP

B

and direction (or the reverse direction in the case of a locomotive running backwards) information packet to each locomotive. Function and lighting information is sent only to the lead locomotive, so only its headlight is lit.

The disadvantage of universal consisting is that when the locomotive reaches the end of its run, you must break the consist and remake it with the last locomotive in the consist as the lead unit. Some systems have a limit on the number of locomotives that can be put in a consist with universal consisting.

A third method of consisting is called advanced consisting. In this method, CV19 is programmed to the same two-digit address in all decoders in the consist. When a non-zero number is programmed into CV19, the decoder responds not only to its active address (either the two-digit address in CV1 or the four-digit address in CVs 17 and 18, whichever is selected by CV29), but the two-digit address programmed into CV19.

You can't use the same two-digit address for an individual locomotive and a consist, otherwise the single unit will respond to the information packet sent to the consist. I don't use two-digit addresses on my layout, and my DCC system remembers which two-digit consist addresses I've used, so I don't

have to worry about this. However, advanced consisting can make lighting a bit more difficult.

Since the same address in the DCC information packets are sent to all decoders in the consist, all of the locomotives will respond to functions in the same way. Packets sent to the locomotive's non-consist address still control its functions.

Having all of the locomotives respond to the consist address is an advantage if only one unit has sound, as the horn and bell will sound no matter where the engine is in the lash-up. When it comes to lighting, having all units respond to the consist address can be a disadvantage.

One tedious option is to select each locomotive individually, set its lighting, and then run the consist. This is where CV21 and CV22 (not available in all decoders) come to the rescue. Configuration Variable 22 controls whether a locomotive's headlights respond to an information packet sent to the consist address. Configuration Variable 21 controls whether or not the locomotive responds to the F1 through F8 function packets.

Computer interface

The specifics are a bit beyond the scope of this book, but there are computer systems available to aid in programming

the more complex CVs. This software runs on an ordinary PC and controls your DCC system. Along with programming CVs, computers can be used to control signal systems, Centralized Traffic Control panels, and many other things.

Some sort of interface is required between your command station and computer. Some DCC systems have a computer interface built in (CVP and NCE are two examples of this type) and some require additional hardware (such as Digitrax, Lenz, and MRC).

If your DCC system requires a separate computer interface, it most likely connects to the cab bus and then to the computer itself. Matching the computer to the software and its interface to the DCC system might require a bit of research. Some of the DCC computer interfaces require an RS-232 serial connection to the computer. It is becoming increasing difficult to find a new computer with an RS-232 interface. There are, however, RS-232 to USB adapters that can be used to interface to newer computers with USB ports.

It might be tempting to use an older computer with an RS-232 port, but be aware that some computer programs will not run on older operating systems. It is best to check the minimum system requirements of the software you are planning to use.

CHAPTER SEVEN

Converting an existing DC layout to DCC

Changing a layout from DC to DCC doesn't have to involve a lot of extra wiring—in fact, most of what you'll need should already be in place.

Chances are if your layout worked well with DC or other command control, it will work fine with DCC, and conversion to DCC will be quick and easy. However, if you have existing electrical problems, DCC won't fix them.

When you begin the process of converting from DC to DCC, it's tempting to try to run both on the same layout at the same time by swapping the DCC system in place of one of the cab-control power packs. However, I don't recommend it. If a locomotive accidentally bridges the gap between a DC and DCC section (and it will), something will likely be damaged—either the DC power pack or the DCC system (and possibly your locomotive too).

The cost of a few extra decoders is not much compared to the cost of replacing a ruined DCC system. Besides, once you have a few locomotives converted, you'll likely be so pleased with the performance of DCC that you'll quickly convert more.

Starting the conversion

If your layout is wired for block control, remove the DC power packs, wire your DCC booster in place of one of the power packs, **A**, and set all the block toggle switches to that side.

If you need more than one booster, connect one in place of each power pack and set some of the block toggles to each booster. Make sure each of the boosters are in phase as explained in Chapter 3. If you decide to further subdivide your layout with circuit breakers, those too can be added in place of DC throttles and some of the blocks set to the breaker, **B**. Wire the input of the breaker to the booster and the output to the block control switch's input.

If your layout is wired for block control using common-rail wiring, cut gaps in the common rail at the same places that the other rail is gapped so that the end of each block is gapped in both rails. This may require adding a track bus for that rail and adding additional track feeders, but it will prevent unintended ground loops and makes the process of putting the boosters in phase easier. If your block control switches only break one side of the track feeders, that's OK; just wire the other side like a track bus as if it were being wired for DCC in the first place.

Also, make sure that your track wiring is heavy enough to handle the maximum current your booster can supply. As noted in Chapter 3, DCC boosters can supply as little as a couple of amps to 10 or more amps. If your booster has a 10-amp capac-

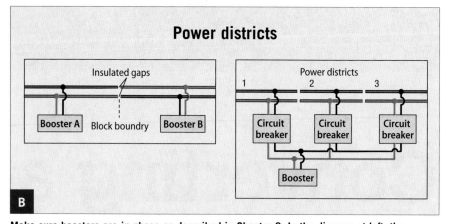

A

Your DCC boosters will take the place of the cab-control DC power packs. Here two boosters are used, each in place of a power pack. If your layout only needs a single booster, all the toggles can simply be switched to that booster.

B

Make sure boosters are in phase as described in Chapter 3. In the diagram at left, the boosters are out of phase. To convert your old electrical blocks into power districts (right), add circuit breakers between the booster and feeders for each block.

ity, you'll need at least 14 AWG bus wiring.

Short runs of wire, like track feeders, can be lighter gauge, so you can likely keep the feeders currently in place on your layout. You may, however, have to add additional track feeders as explained in Chapter 2. Don't forget the "coin test" discussed earlier in the book: place a coin across the rails at various places around the layout to ensure that the booster or circuit breaker detects a short circuit.

If your wires leading from your control panel to the individual blocks are too light, you'll have to replace them with bus wiring as described in Chapter 2.

Turnouts

As discussed in Chapter 4, turnouts that worked fine on a DC layout can sometimes cause trouble on a DCC

layout. The problems were always there, but are more apparent with DCC.

When I first began using DCC, I converted my then-current layout from DC. I had used slide switches under the layout to hold the turnout points in place and switch the frog power. I soon found that if I accidentally ran a locomotive through an open turnout and caused a short circuit, I would have problems with intermittent power to the frog from then on.

I discovered that my slide switches were rated at 3 amps and my booster was rated at 5 amps. All it took was a few instances of short circuits running the full 5 amps through the slide switch, even briefly, to cause the switch to fail. As these switches failed, I replaced them with heavier switches and my problems went away.

List of DCC system and component manufacturers

Atlas Model Railroad Co.
603 Sweetland Ave.
Hillside, NJ 07205
www.atlasrr.com
908-687-0880

Bachmann
1400 E. Erie Ave.
Philadelphia, PA 19124
www.bachmanntrains.com
215-744-4699

CVP Products
P.O. Box 835772
Richardson, TX 75083
www.cvpusa.com
972-422-2169

DCC Specialties
57 River Rd., Ste. 1023
Essex Junction, VT 05452
www.dccspecialties.com
800-671-0641

Digitrax
450 Cemetery St., No. 206
Norcross, GA 30071-4228
www.digitrax.com
770-441-7992

**Electronic Solutions Ulm
(ESU, LokSound)**
112 Pine Ave. E
P.O. Box 77
Upsala, MN 56384
www.loksound.com

**Java Model Railroad Interface
(JMRI, DecoderPro)**
jmri.sourceforge.net

KAM Industries
2373 NW 185th Ave.
Hillsboro, OR 97124
www.kamind.com
503-291-1221

Lenz Agency
P.O. Box 143
Chelmsford, MA 01824
www.lenz.com
978-250-1494

Logic Rail Technologies
21175 Tomball Pkwy., Ste. 287
Houston, TX 77070
www.logicrailtech.com
281-251-5813

Micro-Mark
340 Snyder Ave.
Berkeley Heights, NJ 07922-1595
www.micromark.com
800-225-1066

Miniatronics
561-K Acorn St.
Deer Park, NY 11729
www.miniatronics.com
800-942-9439

Model Rectifier Corp. (MRC)
80 Newfield Ave.
Edison, NJ 08837
www.modelrec.com
732-225-6360

NCE Corp.
899 Ridge Rd.
Webster, NY 14580
www.ncedcc.com
585-671-0370

QSI Solutions
c/o American Hobby Distributors
57 River Rd., Ste. 1023
Essex Junction, VT 05452
www.qsisolutions.com

SoundTraxx
210 Rock Point Dr.
Durango, CO 81301
www.soundtraxx.com
970-259-0690

Southern Digital
5295 Hwy. 78, Ste. D-322
Stone Mountain, GA 30087
www.sodigi.com
770-929-1888

Tony's Train Exchange
Pinewood Plaza
57 River Rd.
P.O. Box 1023
Essex Junction, VT 05452
www.tonystrains.com
800-978-3472

Train Control Systems (TCS)
P.O. Box 341
845 Blooming Glen Rd.
Blooming Glen, PA 18911
www.tcsdcc.com

Tools for a DCC Workshop

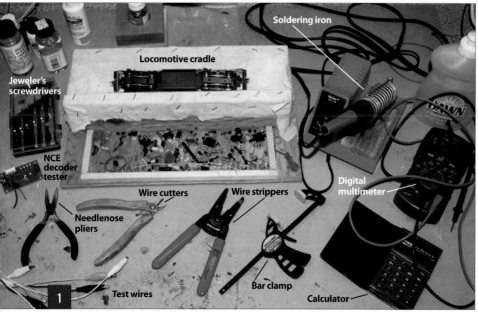

Dedicated workspace. I have a bench in my shop that I'm able to devote to working on Digital Command Control projects. I use an assortment of tools and supplies to install and test decoders.

Test track. Before and after installing a decoder, I try out locomotives on a test track. I have both an HO scale track for my Soo Line layout and an N scale track for my son's Wisconsin Central model railroad.

Installing Digital Command Control

(DCC) decoders and wiring a DCC layout is much easier with the right tools. Some of the tools mentioned here are necessities, while others are needed only for complicated tasks. No matter what the situation, all of these tools will make your next DCC-related project easier.

The basics. You should have a dedicated workspace and a test track for even the simplest decoder installation.

Having a dedicated workspace helps keep tools and supplies organized, **1**.

A test track is essential for testing locomotives before and after installing a de-

coder. My test track, **2**, is at the back of my workbench. It contains sections of HO and N scale track. It can be powered by a variety of sources, including a DC power pack or my DCC system's programming track and main line buses.

I use the DC power pack for testing locomotives prior to installing a decoder, making sure the model runs smoothly in both directions and that all of the lights work. I also measure the locomotive's current draw so I can select the correct decoder.

Before I install the decoder, I use a tester to make sure it works. I use a commercial tester from NCE, although testers are also available from Digitrax, ESU, and Ulrich.

For information on building your own decoder tester, read Bill Darnaby's article "Installing sound decoders in steam engines" in the June 2001 issue of *Model Railroader*.

I test decoders prior to installation because it saves a lot of time that otherwise would be wasted installing and debugging a bad decoder.

Tool time. Even the simplest drop-in decoder installation will require a set of jeweler's screwdrivers. To protect the locomotive from damage while removing screws, it's a good idea to have a locomotive cradle. My son made the cradle shown in **1** out of wood and cloth as part of a Cub Scout project. Commercial cradles made of foam are available, or you can make your own.

An assortment of hand tools makes decoder installation easier. A quality pair of needlenose pliers is ideal for holding small parts and forming wire.

I also recommend wire strippers that are compatible with 30- to 22 AWG wire. For layout wiring, get a pair that will strip wire to the gauge of your track bus.

You'll also want a good pair of wire cutters. Don't use the cutters for anything but cutting copper wire, or they'll quickly be gouged and ruined.

To make electrical connections, you'll need a low-wattage pencil-type soldering iron. A soldering station with an adjustable temperature, an iron holder, and a wet sponge is ideal. I use .032" rosin-core solder for most decoder projects.

Crunching the numbers. There are a variety of tools I keep at my work station for calculating values. The most basic are a pencil, notepad, and calculator. I use these to calculate the value of dropping resistors or configuration variables (CVs).

For more advanced installations, you might find it handy to have a computer. I'm finding that a PC, **3**, is almost a necessity for programming sound and non-sound decoders. I also use the Internet to download sound files and DCC manuals and to update programming software.

Several firms, including Digitrax, ESU, and QSI Solutions, have dedicated hardware for programming their decoders with a computer. I use a rotary switch to control which programmer is connected to my test track.

I also use programming track boosters for programming sound decoders (mentioned in Chapter 6). I have boosters from

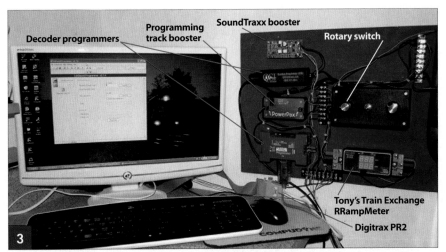

Modern necessities. A PC and several decoder programmers make it easy to customize both sound and non-sound decoders. A rotary switch selects which programmer is connected to the test track.

Labels on image 1: Decoder programmers; Programming track booster; SoundTraxx booster; Rotary switch; Tony's Train Exchange RRampMeter; Digitrax PR2

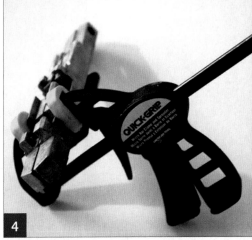

Clamped together. A bar clamp holds the halves of a split locomotive frame together when making cuts.

DCC Specialties and SoundTraxx connected to my programming track rotary switch. The boosters work equally well, so only one should be required.

I keep a digital multimeter (DMM) on hand for measuring voltage, current, and resistance. The meter should be capable of measuring up to 20 volts (V) AC and DC and current up to 1 amp (A), or higher for larger scales.

To easily determine the voltage and current of the DCC signal, I use a RRampMeter from Tony's Train Exchange. I also use the device to measure DC current draw before installing a decoder and DCC current draw afterward. The RRampMeter measures DCC voltage as well, which helps me troubleshoot problems that might occur on my test track.

When making temporary electrical connections, I use a set of test wires with alligator clips. These can be found at RadioShack and other electrical supply stores. Make sure the metal clips don't make unwanted connections that may cause a short circuit.

I use a static mat to control static electricity. Even a small "zap" of static electricity can shorten the life of a decoder.

Making the cuts. When installing a decoder, you may need to modify the locomotive's frame. To make clean, quick cuts, I use a motor tool with a cut-off disk. Wear proper eye and ear protection when using this tool. Also, remove the motor before cutting the frame and keep metal filings away from the decoder, motor, and gears. A

miniature bar clamp, **4**, is useful for holding the split frames of N scale locomotives when cutting and filing.

When I need precise measurements for cutting, I use a set of calipers. They make it easier to measure the inside of a locomotive shell. This is essential when portions of a locomotive frame must be removed to make the decoder fit.

The supply drawer. In addition to the tools already mentioned, I have a well-stocked multi-drawer parts organizer, **5**. What do I keep in all of these drawers? For starters, I keep a variety of small-gauge wires in various sizes and colors. These come in handy for splicing decoder wires. Digitrax offers a pack of 30AWG wire in nine colors.

I also have an assortment of light-emitting diodes (LEDs) and miniature light bulbs. I keep these around in case a light doesn't work or I want to replace a bulb with an LED or vice versa.

Along the lighting theme, I keep a variety of resistors, generally between 100 and 1K Ω, both ¼ and ½ watt.

In addition, I have rolls of electrical tape and double-sided foam tape. The former is for insulating decoders; the latter is for mounting them. I sometimes use poster putty to secure a decoder.

To insulate soldered electrical connections, I have a selection of heat-shrink tubing handy. A heat gun or hair dryer can be used to shrink the tubing. Use these heating devices carefully, as it's easy to accidentally

Supply drawers. Wire, resistors, and light-emitting diodes are just some of the items I keep in my parts organizer. The clear drawers make it easy to see what's inside.

Labels on image 2: Light-emitting diodes; More LEDs; Old decoders; Wire; Light bulbs; Resistors; More resistors; Foam and electrical tape; Poster putty; Spare decoders; Old light boards

melt or distort the plastic shell or fine details on your locomotive.

Finally, I keep a AA battery on hand. I use this to test the 1.5V bulbs found in many locomotives.

I didn't start out with all these items in my workshop. However, I realize installing decoders would have been much easier if I had these items when I first made the switch to DCC. As you gain more experience with DCC, you'll find many of these tools and techniques to be handy.

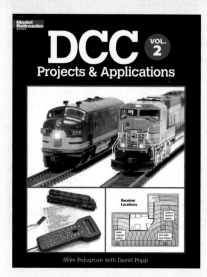
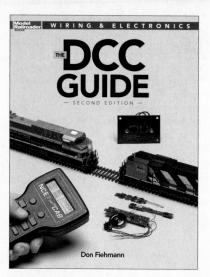
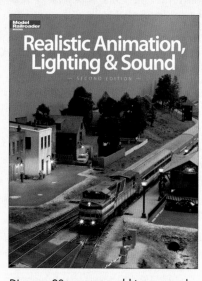